Editor
Amethyst W. Gaidelis, M.A.

Contributing Editor
Tracie I. Heskett, M. Ed.

Illustrator
Clint McKnight

Cover Artist
Tony Carrillo

Art Coordinator
Renée Mc Elwee

Editor in Chief
Ina Massler Levin, M.A.

Creative Director
Karen J. Goldfluss, M.S. Ed.

Imaging
Leonard P. Swierski

Publisher

Mary D. Smith, M.S. Ed.

Summertime Learning

Prepare Your Child for Eighth Grade

TCR 8848

With 8 weeks worth of reading, writing, math and just plain fun!

Also includes:
- Science
- Social Studies
- Test Practice

Teacher Created Resources

M000107466

Teacher Created Resources
6421 Industry Way
Westminster, CA 92683
www.teachercreated.com
ISBN: 978-1-4206-8848-1
©2012 Teacher Created Resources
Reprinted, 2012 (PO5560)
Made in U.S.A.

Teacher Created Resources

Table of Contents

A Message from the National Summer Learning Association. 4
How to Use This Book 5
Standards and Skills. 6
Keeping Track 10
Week 1: Activities 11–20

Monday	Math: *Change for a Dollar*
	Reading: *Running to Win*
Tuesday	Science: *Weight of a World*
	Writing: *Developing Your Ideas*
Wednesday	Math: *Boyd's Home Inspection*
	Reading: *Just Like New!*
Thursday	Social Studies: *Landmarks*
	Writing: *Sentence Possibilities*
Friday	Test-Taking Practice: *Nonfiction Passage*
	Friday Fun: *Rhyming Pairs*

Week 2: Activities 21–30

Monday	Math: *Elliott's Auto Sales*
	Writing: *Learning About Myself*
Tuesday	Social Studies: *Mayan Writing*
	Reading: *The Pied Piper*
Wednesday	Math: *Probability Puzzles*
	Writing: *Then and Now*
Thursday	Science: *Earth's Geologic Plates*
	Reading: *Curfews and Fires*
Friday	Test-Taking Practice: *Verb Tense*
	Friday Fun: *Coded Message*

Week 3: Activities 31–40

Monday	Math: *Service in the Park*
	Reading: *The Zoo of Friendly Living*
Tuesday	Science: *Powerful Predators*
	Writing: *Show, Don't Tell*
Wednesday	Math: *Hidden Art*
	Reading: *Paul Revere's Ride*
Thursday	Social Studies: *Illuminated Ideas*
	Writing: *The Heart of an Essay*
Friday	Test-Taking Practice: *Word Problems*
	Friday Fun: *Things in Common*

Week 4: Activities 41–50

Monday	Math: *Roman Numerals in Modern Times*
	Writing: *Story Parts*
Tuesday	Social Studies: *Cambodia*
	Reading: *Alien Activities*
Wednesday	Math: *Fun Fractions*
	Writing: *Sentence Combining*
Thursday	Science: *Brownian Motion*
	Reading: *Fishing Rods and Triangles*
Friday	Test-Taking Practice: *Describing Motion*
	Friday Fun: *Word Winders*

Week 5: Activities 51–60

Monday	Math: *Bob's Deli*
	Reading: *Vanilla*
Tuesday	Science: *The Amazing Hand*
	Writing: *Sentence Ingredients*

Table of Contents
(cont.)

Week 5: Activities *(cont.)*
    Wednesday   Math: *Favorite Flavors*
                        Reading: *Surviving the Storm*
    Thursday   Social Studies: *Native American Words*
                        Writing: *Fitting More into Sentences*
    Friday   Test-Taking Practice: *Essay Writing*
                        Friday Fun: *Hidden Meanings*

Week 6: Activities 61–70
    Monday   Math: *Challenge*
                        Writing: *Using a Hook*
    Tuesday   Social Studies: *Fun in the Colonies*
                        Reading: *Rat's Discussion*
    Wednesday   Math: *From Graph to Picture*
                        Writing: *The Whole Story*
    Thursday   Science: *Compounds*
                        Reading: *Where Did Spider-Man Come From?*
    Friday   Test-Taking Practice: *Show Your Work*
                        Friday Fun: *Author Puzzle*

Week 7: Activities 71–80
    Monday   Math: *Metric Fun*
                        Reading: *A Preposterous Tale*
    Tuesday   Science: *Rock and Roll*
                        Writing: *Great Examples*
    Wednesday   Math: *Sam's Market*
                        Reading: *Riddles*
    Thursday   Social Studies: *Up From Slavery*
                        Writing: *Plotting a Story*
    Friday   Test-Taking Practice: *Reading Comprehension*
                        Friday Fun: *Mind Benders*

Week 8: Activities 81–90
    Monday   Math: *Triangle Experiment*
                        Writing: *What If?*
    Tuesday   Social Studies: *Morse Code*
                        Reading: *Scorpion Studies*
    Wednesday   Math: *Another Dimension*
                        Writing: *Being Argumentative*
    Thursday   Science: *Lifesaving Blood*
                        Reading: *Stepping Into the Wilderness*
    Friday   Test-Taking Practice: *Locating Information*
                        Friday Fun: *Family Vacation*

All About Me 91
Summer Reading List 92
Fun Ways to Love Books 95
Math Resource: Graph Paper 96
Science Resource: Science Investigation Worksheet 97
Journal Topics 98
Learning Experiences 99
Websites 100
Commonly Misspelled Words 102
Proofreading Marks 103
Measurement Tools 104
Test-Taking Tips 105
Book Review 106
Answer Key 107

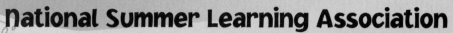

A Message From the
National Summer Learning Association

Dear Parents,

Did you know that all young people experience learning losses when they don't engage in educational activities during the summer? That means some of what they've spent time learning over the preceding school year evaporates during the summer months. However, summer learning loss is something that you can help prevent. Summer is the perfect time for fun and engaging activities that can help children maintain and improve their academic skills. Here are just a few:

- Encourage your son or daughter to read every day. Let your child see you reading every day. Visit the local library frequently to select new books.

- Ask your child's teacher for recommendations of books for summer reading or check with the local librarian. The Summer Reading List in this publication is a good start.

- Explore parks, nature preserves, museums, and cultural centers.

- Consider every day to be a day full of teachable moments. Teach your child to read a map before a car trip and then let him or her be the navigator on your next trip. Plant a vegetable garden and talk about good nutrition as you make a salad together. Use the Learning Experiences in the back of this book for more ideas.

- Each day, set goals to accomplish. For example, choose a current news story and follow it together. Talk about it from various angles. Find articles in the newspaper and online. Have your son or daughter compare the various types of media.

- Encourage your child to complete the activities in books, such as *Summertime Learning*, to help bridge the summer learning gap.

Our vision is for every child to be safe, healthy, and engaged in learning during the summer. Learn more at *www.summerlearning.org* and *www.summerlearningcampaign.org*.

Have a *memorable* summer.

Matthew C. Boulay
Interim CEO
National Summer Learning Association

How to Use This Book

As a parent, you know that summertime is a time for fun and learning. So it is quite handy that fun and learning can go hand in hand when your child uses *Summertime Learning*.

Book Organization

Summertime Learning is organized around an eight-week summer vacation period. For each weekday, there are two lessons, an English lesson and a math, science, or social studies lesson. Fridays feature a Test-Taking Practice page and a Friday Fun activity.

The calendar looks like this:

Day	Week 1	Week 2	Week 3	Week 4	Week 5	Week 6	Week 7	Week 8
M	Math Reading	Math Writing	Math Reading	Math Writing	Math Reading	Math Writing	Math Reading	Math Writing
T	Science Writing	Social Studies Reading	Science Writing	Social Studies Reading	Science Writing	Social Studies Reading	Science Writing	Social Studies Reading
W	Math Reading	Math Writing	Math Reading	Math Writing	Math Reading	Math Writing	Math Reading	Math Writing
T	Social Studies Writing	Science Reading	Social Studies Writing	Science Reading	Social Studies Writing	Science Reading	Social Studies Writing	Science Reading
F	Test-Taking Practice Friday Fun	Test-Taking Practice Friday Fun	Test-Taking Practice Friday Fun	Test-Taking Practice Friday Fun	Test-Taking Practice Friday Fun	Test-Taking Practice Friday Fun	Test-Taking Practice Friday Fun	Test-Taking Practice Friday Fun

There are many ways to use this book effectively with your child. We list three ideas here.

Day by Day: You can have your child do the activities in order, beginning on the first Monday of summer vacation. The pages are designed so that each day's lessons are back to back on a page. The book is also perforated so you can tear the pages out for your child to work on. If you opt to have your child tear out the pages, you might want to store the completed pages in a special folder or three-ring binder that your child personalizes.

Pick and Choose: You may find that you do not want to have your child work strictly in order. Feel free to pick and choose any combination of pages based on your child's needs and interests.

All of a Kind: Perhaps your child needs more help in one content area than another. You may opt to have him or her work only in that area.

Keeping Track

A "Keeping Track" chart is included on page 10 of this book. On completion of a page have your child fill in the blanks. He or she might enjoy coming up with a code to represent each type of activity. If desired, you may wish to have your child work towards agreed-upon rewards for a certain number of pages completed.

Standards and Skills

Standards and Skills

Each activity in *Summertime Learning* meets one or more of the following strategies and skills.* The activities in this book are designed to help your child reinforce the skills learned during seventh grade, as well as introduce new skills that will be learned in eighth grade.

Language Arts Standards
- ✿ Uses the general skills and strategies of the writing process
- ✿ Uses the stylistic and rhetorical aspects of writing
- ✿ Uses grammatical and mechanical conventions in written composition
- ✿ Uses the general skills and strategies of the reading process
- ✿ Uses skills and strategies to read a variety of literary texts
- ✿ Uses skills and strategies to read a variety of informational texts

Mathematics Standards
- ✿ Uses a variety of strategies in the problem-solving process
- ✿ Understands and applies basic and advanced properties of the concepts of numbers
- ✿ Uses basic and advanced procedures while performing the processes of computation
- ✿ Understands and applies basic and advanced properties of the concepts of measurement
- ✿ Understands and applies basic and advanced properties of the concepts of geometry
- ✿ Understands and applies basic and advanced concepts of probability
- ✿ Understands and applies basic and advanced properties of functions and algebra

Social Studies Standards
- ✿ Understands the characteristics and uses of maps, globes, and other geographic tools and technologies
- ✿ Knows the location of places, geographic features, and patterns of the environment
- ✿ Understands the characteristics and uses of spatial organization of Earth's surface
- ✿ Understands the physical and human characteristics of place
- ✿ Understands the concept of regions
- ✿ Understands the characteristics of ecosystems on Earth's surface
- ✿ Understands the nature and complexity of Earth's cultural mosaics
- ✿ Understands the patterns of human settlement and their causes
- ✿ Understands the forces of cooperation and conflict that shape the divisions of Earth's surface
- ✿ Understands how physical systems affect human systems
- ✿ Understands how geography is used to interpret the past
- ✿ Understands and knows how to analyze chronological relationships and patterns
- ✿ Understands the historical perspective

Science Standards
- ✿ Understands Earth's composition and structure
- ✿ Understands the structure and function of cells and organisms
- ✿ Understands relationships among organisms and their physical environment

Standards and Skills (cont.)

Science Standards (cont.)

- ☼ Understands the structure and properties of matter
- ☼ Understands forces and motion
- ☼ Understands the scientific enterprise

Writing Skills

- ☼ Uses a variety of strategies to draft and revise written work
- ☼ Uses a variety of strategies to edit and publish written work
- ☼ Evaluates own and others' writing
- ☼ Uses style, content, and structure appropriate for specific audiences and purposes
- ☼ Writes expository compositions
- ☼ Uses descriptive language that clarifies and enhances ideas
- ☼ Uses paragraph form in writing
- ☼ Uses a variety of sentence structures to expand and imbed ideas
- ☼ Uses nouns, pronouns, verbs, adjectives, adverbs, prepositions and coordinating conjunctions in written compositions
- ☼ Uses conventions of spelling, capitalization, and punctuation in written compositions

Reading Skills

- ☼ Establishes and adjusts purposes for reading
- ☼ Uses a variety of strategies to extend reading vocabulary
- ☼ Understands level-appropriate reading vocabulary
- ☼ Reads a variety of literary passages and texts
- ☼ Understands complex elements of plot development
- ☼ Understands elements of character development
- ☼ Understands point of view in a literary text
- ☼ Makes connections between characters or the causes for complex events in texts and those in his or her own life
- ☼ Reads a variety of informational texts
- ☼ Knows the defining structural characteristics and features used in informational texts
- ☼ Summarizes and paraphrases information in texts
- ☼ Uses new information to adjust and extend personal knowledge base
- ☼ Draws conclusions and makes inferences based on explicit and implicit information in texts

Mathematics Skills

- ☼ Understands how to break a complex problem into simpler parts or use a similar problem type to solve a problem
- ☼ Uses a variety of strategies to understand problem-solving situations and processes
- ☼ Formulates a problem, determines information required to solve the problem, chooses methods for obtaining this information, and sets limits for acceptable solutions

Standards and Skills (cont.)

Mathematics Skills (cont.)

✿ Understands the role of written symbols in representing mathematical ideas and the use of precise language in conjunction with the special symbols of mathematics
✿ Understands the relationships among equivalent number representations and the advantages and disadvantages of each type of representation
✿ Understands the role of positive and negative integers in the number system
✿ Understands the characteristics and uses of exponents and scientific notation
✿ Understands the concepts of ratio, proportion, and percent and the relationships among them
✿ Adds, subtracts, multiplies, and divides integers and rational numbers
✿ Adds and subtracts fractions with unlike denominators; multiplies and divides fractions
✿ Uses proportional reasoning to solve mathematical and real-world problems
✿ Understands the properties of operations with rational numbers
✿ Understands the basic concept of rate as a measure
✿ Solves problems involving perimeter (circumference) and area of various shapes
✿ Understands the relationships among linear dimensions, area, and volume and the corresponding uses of units, square units, and cubic units of measure
✿ Solves problems involving units of measurement and converts answers to a larger or smaller unit within the same system
✿ Understands formulas for finding measures
✿ Understands the defining properties of triangles
✿ Reads and interprets data in charts, tables, and plots
✿ Uses data and statistical measures for a variety of purposes
✿ Determines probability using mathematical/theoretical models
✿ Understands how predictions are based on data and probabilities
✿ Understands various representations of patterns and functions and the relationships among them
✿ Solves linear equations using concrete, informal, and formal methods
✿ Understands basic operations on algebraic expressions

Social Studies Skills

✿ Uses thematic maps
✿ Knows how maps help to find patterns of movement in space and time
✿ Knows the location of physical and human features on maps and globes
✿ Knows how mental maps can reflect attitudes and perceptions of places
✿ Understands the patterns and processes of migration and diffusion
✿ Knows the human characteristics of places
✿ Knows the physical characteristics of places
✿ Knows regions at various spatial scales
✿ Understands criteria that give a region identity
✿ Knows types of regions such as formal regions, functional regions, and perceptual regions
✿ Knows changes that have occurred over time in ecosystems in the local region

Standards and Skills (cont.)

Social Studies Skills (cont.)

- ✿ Knows the distinctive cultural landscapes associated with migrant populations
- ✿ Knows the similarities and differences in various settlement patterns of the world
- ✿ Knows the factors involved in the development of cities
- ✿ Understands the various factors involved in the development of nation-states
- ✿ Understands the factors that affect the cohesiveness and integration of countries
- ✿ Knows the ways in which human systems develop in response to conditions in the physical environment
- ✿ Knows how the physical environment affects life in different regions
- ✿ Knows the ways people take aspects of the environment into account when deciding on locations for human activities
- ✿ Knows the ways in which humans prepare for natural hazards
- ✿ Knows the ways in which the spatial organization of society changes over time
- ✿ Understands patterns of change and continuity in the historical succession of related events
- ✿ Analyzes the influence specific ideas and beliefs had on a period of history

Science Skills

- ✿ Knows that the Earth is comprised of layers including a core, mantle, lithosphere, hydrosphere, and atmosphere
- ✿ Knows that the Earth's crust is divided into plates that move at extremely slow rates in response to movements in the mantle
- ✿ Knows that all organisms are composed of cells, which are the fundamental units of life; most organisms are single cells, but other organisms (including humans) are multi-cellular
- ✿ Knows how an organism's ability to regulate its internal environment enables the organism to obtain and use resources, grow, reproduce, and maintain stable internal conditions while living in a constantly changing external environment
- ✿ Knows ways in which organisms interact and depend on one another through food chains and food webs in an ecosystem
- ✿ Knows that matter is made up of tiny particles called atoms, and different arrangements of atoms into groups compose all substances
- ✿ Knows that elements often combine to form compounds (e.g., molecules, crystals)
- ✿ Knows that an object's motion can be described and represented graphically according to its position, direction of motion, and speed
- ✿ Knows that people of all backgrounds and with diverse interests, talents, qualities, and motivations engage in fields of science and engineering; some of these people work in teams and others work alone, but all communicate extensively with others
- ✿ Knows ways in which science and society influence one another

* Standards and skills used with permission from McREL (Copyright 2011, McREL. Midcontinent Research for Education and Learning. Address: 4601 DTC Boulevard, Suite 500, Denver, CO 80237. Telephone: 303-337-0990. Website: www.mcrel. org/standards-benchmarks). To align McREL Standards to the Common Core Standards, go to www.mcrel.org.

Change for a Dollar

Math

There are over 100 ways to make change for a dollar. How many ways can you find?

Directions: Find as many coin combinations as you can. Each one must equal a dollar. List the coins in order on each line, from greatest value to smallest value. The list has been started for you.

> **Abbreviations**
>
> p = penny   n = nickel   d = dime   q = quarter   hd = half dollar

2 hd

1 hd, 2 q

1 hd, 5 d

1 hd, 10 n

Running to Win

What was called "the most daring move ever seen on a track" occurred on August 4, 1936, in Berlin, Germany. The "move" was performed by John Woodruff, a black American competitor, in the middle of the 800-meter running race at the 1936 Olympic Games. Young and inexperienced, Woodruff was only a 21-year-old college freshman when he earned his spot on the United States Olympic team.

At the start of the race, the 6-foot 3-inch (2 m) tall Woodruff became trapped, boxed in by the more experienced runners. All the spectators assumed Woodruff would lose. He was surrounded, and if he broke between the two leaders, he would be disqualified with a foul. Woodruff may have been an inexperienced novice, but he was a quick thinker. He made a decision, and as the crowd gasped in disbelief, he acted on it.

Woodruff came to a complete stop. After waiting until all the other runners in the pack had passed him, he quickly moved to an outside lane. Once alone and in the outer lane, Woodruff charged for the winner's tape that stretched across the finish line. As the roars of the astonished crowd filled the stadium, Woodruff extended his stride so that it measured nearly 10 feet (3 m), and with a burst of speed he took the lead. Woodruff was victorious, with a winning time of 1 minute, 52.9 seconds.

Directions: Answer the following questions based on the passage.

1. One could say that when Woodruff made his move, it was like giving the other runners
   a. a foul.
   b. an affront.
   c. a head start.
   d. a spot in an outer lane.

2. From this story, one can learn that
   a. runners can be disqualified.
   b. only daring runners win gold medals.
   c. runners always want the inside lane.
   d. older runners have an edge over younger runners.

3. Tell what the numbers mentioned in the story "Running to Win" refer to.

   4 _____   6' 3" _____

   1936 _____   10 _____

   21 _____   1:52.9 _____

Challenge: Imagine "Running to Win" is a newspaper article and you need to come up with a new title for it. Write down a headline that gives readers a good idea of what they will learn in the article. Your headline must be less than 10 words long.

Weight of a World

When you step on a scale, it measures how powerfully Earth's gravity is pulling on you. Your weight is expressed in pounds. The surface gravity of each planet, moon, or object in the solar system is different. Some planets have a greater gravitational pull than Earth. Others have less. This chart shows the surface gravity on each planet. Earth has a 1 and is the basis of comparison for all other planets.

Planet	Surface Gravity	Percent
Mercury	0.38	38%
Venus	0.91	91%
Earth	1.00	100%
Mars	0.38	38%
Jupiter	2.36	236%
Saturn	0.92	92%
Uranus	0.89	89%
Neptune	1.12	112%

Directions: Estimate the weight of an object. Then, multiply the weight times the surface gravity of each planet listed above. Use the decimal to multiply.

Example: 100 pounds x 0.38 surface gravity = 38 pounds (weight on Mercury)

Estimate the weight of a large watermelon or pumpkin. Calculate its weight on each planet. List your answers on this chart.

Now choose something much heavier, like a piece of furniture or a large boulder. Compute the weight of this new object on each planet.

Planet	Weight
Mercury	_____
Venus	_____
Earth	_____
Mars	_____
Jupiter	_____
Saturn	_____
Uranus	_____
Neptune	_____

Planet	Weight
Mercury	_____
Venus	_____
Earth	_____
Mars	_____
Jupiter	_____
Saturn	_____
Uranus	_____
Neptune	_____

Challenge: The moon's surface gravity is 0.17. What would each object weigh on the moon? Pluto's surface gravity is 0.06. What would each object weigh on Pluto?

Developing Your Ideas

Many authors draw on past experiences when they are writing. Reread a passage from a favorite book. Think about what experiences the author might have used from his or her own life when writing this passage.

What interesting experiences happened in your past? Do you have any relatives who said or did odd things? How did you react? Think of a time when something unusual happened in your family just because one person acted a certain way.

Directions: Brainstorm unique family situations. Then write about a specific event. You may add extra fictional details if you like. If you need a starter, use the following prompt:

"When _____ came to visit, _____."
               (a relative)   (the event that happened)

_____

_____

_____

_____

_____

_____

_____

_____

_____

_____

_____

_____

Read what you wrote. How did you incorporate relevant details? Have you included too much unnecessary information?

Challenge: Think of a sport you would like to try. On another piece of paper, draw a picture showing a character playing that sport. Then write a story about the character's (your) adventure.

Ideas: rock climbing, surfing, curling, discus, croquet, shot put, lawn bowling, water polo

Boyd's Home Inspection

Boyd is a home inspector. He also does minor installations. The larger the room that he must inspect, the more he charges for his services. When he is asked to inspect a room, the first thing that he must do is find the area and perimeter. He uses this information to calculate individual prices for his services.

Directions: Complete the input/output tables and answer the questions.

Part I

Complete the following table to help Boyd. The sizes for the rooms that he will measure will increase by equal amounts. Figure out the equal amount that the room increases by and use that amount to calculate the measurements of the other rooms. You will develop a rule and that rule will help you make all of the other calculations.

Rule: _____

Input: x	Output: y
540 sq. feet	$1,080
600 sq. feet	$1,200
660 sq. feet	
720 sq. feet	
780 sq. feet	

For this input/output table, the input (x) is equal to the area of the room and the output (y) is equal to the service price.

1. What steps did you follow in order to determine the rule for the table?

   _____

   _____

2. For the table above, is the statement "x multiplied by 2 is equal to y" true?

Part II

Boyd orders materials for a room based upon its size. He is preparing to install baseboards. This item will be installed around the perimeter of each room. Help him to complete the table.

The rule for the table is given below. Use the rule to complete the pricing guide for baseboard installation.

Rule: Input multiplied by 150% is equal to output

Input: x	Output: y
100 feet	$150
200 feet	$300
300 feet	
400 feet	
500 feet	

For this input/output table, the input (x) is equal to the perimeter of the room and the output (y) is equal to the service price.

1. How much will Boyd and his associates charge to install baseboards for a room that has a 400 ft. perimeter? _____

2. If the client had a room with a perimeter of 150 ft., what would be the baseboard installation price? (Hint: Use the rule from the table to calculate your answer.)

   _____

Just Like New!

Part I

Directions: Fill in the missing words in the advertisement below. Use this glossary to help you.

> **tamper** — to interfere   **decrepit** — broken down
>
> **assure** — to promise   **salvage** — to save from waste
>
> **reserve** — something saved for future use   **furnish** — to give supplies

Computer for Sale!

This unique machine is a homemade computer that I put together from parts of other computers that I was able to (1) _____. The condition is excellent, and I suggest that you not (2) _____ with it. It will serve you well for many years just as it is. Although it is four years old, it is certainly not (3) _____.

My asking price is $250. That's a good deal, I (4) _____ you! If you have a (5) _____ of money, this would be a good way to spend it. Call me at 555-4120. I will even (6) _____ you with a one-of-a-kind printer that I built from scratch!

Part II

Directions: Unscramble the words to spell your new vocabulary words correctly.

pecdrite _____   nurhsif _____

glavsea _____   pratem _____

sevreer _____   serasu _____

Challenge: Fill in the blanks with your new words.

1. The Abbotts keep a _____ of food in case of an emergency.

2. I can _____ you that my friend can be trusted with your money.

3. The Army will _____ the soldiers with weapons.

4. My washing machine is old and _____.

5. Do not _____ with my private journal.

6. Could they _____ anything from the shipwreck?

Landmarks

Directions: Using the landmark names listed in the box, label each landmark. Start with the ones you are sure of and use the process of elimination.

Big Ben	Angkor Wat	Golden Gate Bridge	Great Pyramid of Giza
Taj Mahal	Gateway Arch	Parthenon	Sydney Opera House
	Great Wall	Chichén Itzá	Kremlin

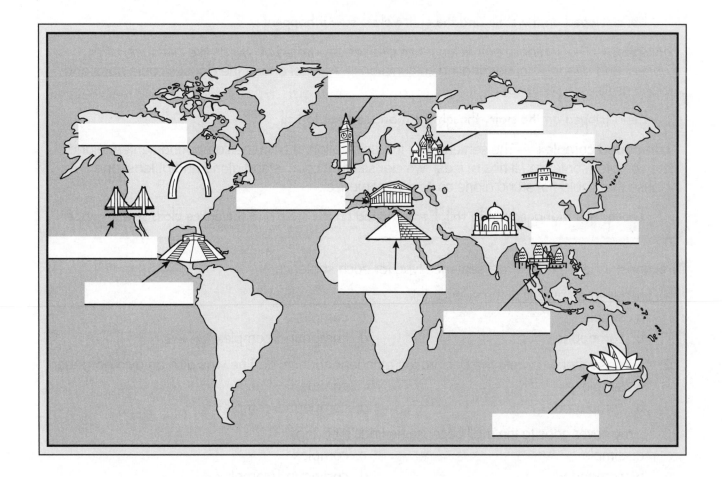

Sentence Possibilities

There are four main types of sentences. Good writers usually use all the types in their writing to vary sentence length and to make the text clear and graceful. Here are the four types of sentences.

> **simple** — The sentence has only one clause.
>
> Lena tripped on the stair.
>
> **compound** — The sentence has at least two clauses separated by words like *and, but,* and *or* (coordinating conjunctions). Each clause could stand alone as its own sentence.
>
> Lena tripped on the stair and the entire class saw it happen.
>
> **complex** — The sentence has at least two clauses separated by words like *because, after, unless,* and *although* (subordinating conjunctions). At least one of the clauses could not stand alone as its own sentence.
>
> Lena tripped on the stair, though she managed not to fall.
>
> **compound complex** — The sentence fits the description of both the compound sentence and the complex sentence. It has at least two clauses that could stand alone and at least one clause that could not stand alone as its own sentence.
>
> Though she managed not to fall, Lena tripped on the stair and the entire class saw it happen.

Directions: Choose the correct sentence type for each sentence.

1. I received an award at the science fair.
   - a. simple
   - b. compound
   - c. complex
   - d. compound/complex

2. Thomas Jefferson wrote the Declaration of Independence, and he was also an avid gardener.
   - a. simple
   - b. compound
   - c. complex
   - d. compound/complex

3. Leroy never goes to the mall because he finds it boring.
   - a. simple
   - b. compound
   - c. complex
   - d. compound/complex

4. Although I love to cook, I am not a very good baker and I tend to burn cookies.
   - a. simple
   - b. compound
   - c. complex
   - d. compound/complex

Challenge: Explain the four sentence types to a friend or family member and give examples. Come up with your own example for each sentence type.

Nonfiction Passage

Directions: Read the passage and then fill in the bubble for the correct answer to each question.

The ground shakes when Earth's crust moves. This is called an *earthquake*. It can be caused by the crust sliding, volcanic bursts, or man-made explosions. Earthquakes that cause the most damage come from the crust sliding.

At first, the crust may only bend because of pushing forces. But when the pushing becomes too much, the crust snaps and shifts into a new position. Shifting makes wiggles of energy that go out in all directions. This is like ripples when a stone is dropped into water. These are called *seismic waves*. The waves travel out from where the center of the earthquake is located. Sometimes people can hear these waves. This is because they make the planet ring like a bell. It must be awesome to hear this sound!

The crust moving may leave a crack, or fault, in the land. Geologists, scientists who study Earth's surface, say that earthquakes often happen where there are old faults, or breaks in the crust. Where there are faults, earthquakes may happen again and again.

Sometimes, when earthquakes happen under the ocean floor, they cause huge sea waves. These waves are called *tsunamis*. They can travel across the ocean as fast as 598 miles per hour. Tsunamis can produce waves over 49 feet high.

Although earthquakes are usually frightening, keep in mind that the distance to the center of Earth is 3,960 miles. Most earthquakes begin less than 150 miles below the surface. Earthquakes are not a sign that Earth is unsteady.

1. Earthquakes are caused by
   ⓐ a giant sound beneath the ground.
   ⓑ explosions and the crust sliding.
   ⓒ volcanoes.
   ⓓ b and c

2. Huge waves that rush across the ocean can be caused by
   ⓐ tsunamis.
   ⓑ storms.
   ⓒ earthquakes beneath the ocean.
   ⓓ waves as high as 49 feet.

3. According to the passage, seismic waves can be compared to
   ⓐ ripples in water.
   ⓑ a bell ringing.
   ⓒ faults in the ground.
   ⓓ none of these

4. The author's purpose in this passage is
   ⓐ to scare the reader.
   ⓑ to inform the reader.
   ⓒ to entertain the reader.
   ⓓ to bore the reader.

5. When earthquakes happen under the ocean floor, they sometimes cause
   ⓐ tidal waves.
   ⓑ jet streams.
   ⓒ tsunamis.
   ⓓ none of the above.

6. You read in the newspaper that an old fault has been discovered nearby. What might happen?
   ⓐ It will swallow you alive.
   ⓑ An earthquake might happen there.
   ⓒ A flood might happen there.
   ⓓ Nothing will happen.

Rhyming Pairs

Directions: Find an adjective that rhymes with a noun so that together, the two words have about the same meaning as the phrase that is given. An example has been done for you.

clever feline   _witty kitty_

bashful insect   _____

obese feline   _____

minor car crash   _____

large swine   _____

ill hen   _____

little snack   _____

enjoyable jogging   _____

soaked dog   _____

bloody tale   _____

ailing bloodsucker   _____

light red beverage   _____

comical rabbit   _____

unhappy boy   _____

Challenge: Come up with more rhyming pairs and make up clues. See if you can get a friend or family member to guess your rhyming pairs.

_____   _____

_____   _____

_____   _____

Elliott's Auto Sales

At Elliott's Auto Sales, Elliott accidentally threw out the receipts for the last six months of business.

Directions: Help Elliott figure out the number of cars that were sold and sales commissions for all of his employees.

Part I

Fill out the table. In order to do so, you must work backwards. Read the information carefully to figure out the car sales for each month. You may have to read the information more than once to complete the table.

March was a good month for car sales because they sold twice the amount they sold in July. They sold the same amount in July and August. April's sales were 20 cars less than in August. Car sales in April and June were the same. In May they sold 70 cars. In August, they sold 25 less than in May.

Six-Month Car Lot Sales Record

March _____

April _____

May _____

June _____

July _____

August _____

Part II

At Elliott's Auto Sales, all of the sales people earn $350.00 a week as their base pay. In addition, they also receive a percentage of the sales price on all of the cars that they sell. Help Elliott figure out how much each person should be paid for the month of September. Complete the table.

Salesperson	Sales Total		Sales Percentage		Monthly Base Pay		Total Amount
Mr. Sanders	$45,000	×	10%	+	$1,400	=	
Ms. Elliott	$20,000	×	5%	+	$1,400	=	
Mrs. Shaw	$50,000	×	10%	+	$1,400	=	
Mr. Smitz	$30,000	×	5%	+	$1,400	=	

Learning About Myself

Directions: Use the quotation to help you answer the questions.

> *"Sometimes it is more important to discover what one cannot do than what one can do."*
>
> ~ Lin Ytuang

1. What does this quote mean to you?_____

_____

2. Why do you think it is important to know your weak traits as well as your strong traits?

_____

_____

3. What do you think is one of your strong traits? _____

4. What do you think is one of your weak traits? _____

5. What is a good way of thinking about your weak traits? _____

_____

Challenge:

There are many different ways of learning. Most people learn from each other, from their experiences, from Internet research, etc. What if everything you learned had to come from a book?

_____

_____

_____

_____

Is there anything that you can only learn from written materials? What?

_____

_____

Mayan Writing

The Mayan civilization was one of the most advanced early civilizations. To learn more about it, archaeologists study the Mayan ruins in Mexico and Central America. They also read the accounts of the Spanish conquistadors and writings of the Mayans themselves.

The Mayans built beautiful cities and studied the stars. They also developed advanced mathematic understandings and created an elaborate writing system. They were meticulous at keeping records. Most of their writing was destroyed, but a few codices, or ancient books, have been found.

In 1697, Spanish conquistadors overtook the last Mayan city, Tayasal. It is said that the people of the city vanished into the forest and were never found, and that they took treasures with them, including a huge library of Mayan scrolls. Archaeological teams have searched for these scrolls and for other writings that might teach us more about this advanced civilization.

Directions: After reading the passage, follow the steps below to create your own glyphs.

Glyphs, unlike letters, are pictograms used to represent whole words or parts of words. Here are a few examples:

person   sun   fire   snake

Now create your own glyphs. They can be pictures that look like the things they represent, or they can be symbols that don't look very similar.

dog   heart   president   bicycle

Now try a few more. These will be harder because they are not animals or objects.

run   sadness   smaller   year

Challenge: On another piece of paper, create a message using your own hieroglyphs.

The Pied Piper

Directions: Read the passage and then choose the best answer to each question.

In Upper Saxony, there is a town called Hamelin. It is located near where two large rivers join together.

Once, this town was infested with rats. There were so many rats that they ate almost all of the food the people had been storing for the winter months. The residents tried to chase away the rats, but nothing they tried worked. One day, a stranger came to Hamelin. He was very tall and wore colorful clothing. He told the townspeople that he would get rid of the rats for a fee, and they agreed.

The stranger took out a flute and began to play. Immediately, all the rats came out of their holes and nests and followed him as he led them to the river. The rats ran into the river and drowned. The stranger returned to the town and asked for his payment, but the townspeople refused to pay him. The next day, when all the adults were busy, the stranger got out another flute and began to play as he again walked towards the river. When the townspeople returned home, they could not find their children. They never saw them again.

1. What does the stranger agree to do?

   a. to rid the town of rats

   b. to play the flute at festivals

   c. to discipline badly behaved children

   d. He doesn't agree to do anything.

2. What part do the townspeople play in the disappearance of the children?

   a. They send the children away to a distant city.

   b. They refuse to pay the stranger.

   c. They have nothing to do with it.

   d. They give the stranger permission to take them to a music school.

3. It is likely that the rats and the children followed the stranger because

   a. they were sleepy.

   b. they liked him.

   c. he gave them magical powers.

   d. he had magical powers.

4. The moral of this story is

   a. don't trust strangers.

   b. honor your debts.

   c. don't live in a town with rats.

   d. don't listen to flute music.

Probability Puzzles

Math

Directions: Use what you know about probability and your common sense to answer these questions.

1. If you spin the spinner once, what is the probability that each of these things will happen? The first one has been done for you.

   a. The spinner will land on 9. The probability is 1 in 12. (written as 1:12 or 1/12)

   b. The spinner will land on a multiple of 2.

   c. The spinner will land on an odd number.

   d. The spinner will land on a prime number.

   e. The spinner will land on a number less than 8.

   f. The spinner will **not** land on 7 or 4.

2. A laundry basket contains 3 red socks, 5 orange socks, 4 blue socks, and 8 black socks. If you pick a sock without looking, what is the probability that each of these things will happen?

   a. You will pick an orange sock.

   b. You will pick a blue sock.

   c. You will **not** pick a blue sock.

   d. You will pick a white sock.

3. If your relatives said you had a 40% chance of going on vacation with them, would you plan on going and pack your clothes?

   How would your actions change if they said you had a 70% chance?

   How would your actions change if they said you had a 95% chance?

Then and Now

Directions: Think of things in your daily life that have changed or been invented since older people in your family were your age. Here are just a few of the areas you can consider:

> communication   music
>
> transportation   first jobs
>
> favorite things to do

Interview an older family member to get information for the "In the Past" part of the chart. Then fill out the "Now" part of the chart with observations from your own life. If you'd like, you can do this in reverse order, starting with the "Now" part of the chart.

Topic:	
In the Past	**Now**

Challenge: Imagine you traveled back in time to when your relative was young. On a separate piece of paper, write a short story describing your experience.

Earth's Geologic Plates

Directions: For this activity, you will need three different colors of pencil, crayon, or pen. Read the passage. Use the three colors to mark or highlight information about the three types of plate boundaries.

Earth's *lithosphere*, its outer shell, is made up of moving plates. There are about 20 of these plates on our planet. Because the plates are resting on top of the molten part of the mantle, they are always moving. Of course, they move slowly and very little, but they move in all different directions.

As the plates move, they create the features that we can see on the crust of Earth. Things like canyons, mountains, and valleys are a result of the constantly moving plates. The study of Earth's plates and the features they produce is called *plate tectonics*.

A plate boundary is the place where two of Earth's plates meet. The plates can move away from each other, move towards each other, or slide past each other. There are three different types of plate boundaries:

- ✿ A transform boundary is when two plates slide past each other.
- ✿ A divergent boundary is when two plates move away from each other.
- ✿ A convergent boundary is when two plates crash into each other.

At transform boundaries, faults are created. A fault is a huge break in the crust of Earth. The San Andreas Fault in California is an example of a transform boundary. At divergent boundaries, large valleys can be formed. The Great Rift Valley in Africa is an example of a spreading valley. At convergent boundaries, mountain ranges can be produced. The Andes Mountains in South America are an example of a convergent boundary.

Challenge: Draw and label an example of each type of boundary.

Curfews and Fires

Directions: Read the passage. Then answer each question.

Laughing, Yow said, "So what happens to us if we aren't home by midnight? Do we turn into mice or pumpkins, or do we lose a shoe?"

Zenaida, the friend Yow was visiting, explained, "There's a town curfew for all teenagers. Unless accompanied by an adult, teenagers have to be off the streets by 10:00 p.m. on school nights and by midnight on weekends."

"That's preposterous!" Yow said. "Isn't that a violation of our civil rights? This is a free country, so we shouldn't be prohibited from using public streets or spaces."

Jonathon, Zenaida's friend, added, "The curfew was voted on and accepted by the majority of the town council, a publicly elected body. It wasn't passed to create disharmony; it was only passed to keep teenagers safe."

Having finished his 48-hour shift, Mr. Montgomery, Zenaida's father and a city firefighter, happened to overhear Jonathon's comment as he walked in the door. He said, "Did you know that the word *curfew* has medieval French origins? In medieval France, the *courvre-feu* or 'cover-fire' was the hour when all the fires in town had to be put out, or at least covered, so people could sleep without fear. Over time, the word metamorphosed into the English 'curfew,' which means the time one needs to be back home or off the streets."

Maggie, an aspiring firefighter and Zenaida's older sister, said, "You can hear French in a word related to firefighting today. Firefighters have to practice *defenestrating* themselves because sometimes in life-or-death situations defenestration is necessary."

"What in the world does *defenestration* mean?" Yow asked.

Maggie replied, "In French, the word for 'window' is *fenetre*. When something is defenestrated, it is thrown out of a window. 'Defenestration' means throwing a person or a thing out of a window."

1. One can tell that Yow could be visiting on a
   a. Monday.
   b. Tuesday.
   c. Thursday.
   d. Saturday.

2. From this story, one can tell that
   a. words from one language may have ties to another.
   b. French firefighters were the first to pass curfews.
   c. Maggie is aspiring to be a specialized smokejumper.
   d. not all firefighters train for life-or-death situations.

3. Take a side: Do you think towns and cities should be allowed to enact curfews for teenagers? Why? Be convincing. _____

_____

_____

_____

_____

Verb Tense

Directions: Identify the underlined verb tense. Make sure to read each sentence carefully, then fill in the bubble that corresponds with the correct answer.

Reminder		Sample
present	grow	The trees <u>were growing</u> quickly because of the climate.
present progressive	is growing	ⓐ past perfect
past	grew	ⓑ past
past progressive	was growing	ⓒ present
future	will grow	🔘 past progressive
future progressive	will be growing	

1. They <u>will be shopping</u> around the clock to get ready for that party.
   ⓐ future
   ⓑ present progressive
   ⓒ past progressive
   ⓓ future progressive

2. Before it started to rain, I <u>was walking</u> to school every day.
   ⓐ present progressive
   ⓑ future progressive
   ⓒ past progressive
   ⓓ past

3. By the end of the food drive, we <u>will be collecting</u> ten pounds of food a day.
   ⓐ future progressive
   ⓑ future
   ⓒ present progressive
   ⓓ present

4. The cat <u>plays</u> with the yarn as his owner laughs.
   ⓐ present
   ⓑ present progressive
   ⓒ future progressive
   ⓓ future

5. I <u>am exercising</u> to keep healthy.
   ⓐ present
   ⓑ present progressive
   ⓒ future progressive
   ⓓ past progressive

6. I <u>will sing</u> in the talent show two weeks from now.
   ⓐ present progressive
   ⓑ future progressive
   ⓒ future
   ⓓ past progressive

Directions: Solve each riddle below. Then use the letters you have circled to reveal a famous saying. If you are unsure of some answers, figuring out the saying can help you.

7	1	4	9	5	3	11	2	7	1	4

8	6	11	3	10	7	1	4	9	5	3

1. If your mother's sister is your aunt, circle **O**. If not, circle **A**.

2. If a prairie dog is a dog, circle **K**. If it's a rodent, circle **F**.

3. If 6 x 6 is 35, circle **M**. If not, circle **N**.

4. If the capital of Nevada is Reno, circle **Y**. If not, circle **U**.

5. If John F. Kennedy is one of the four famous faces carved on Mt. Rushmore, circle **K**. If not, circle **A**.

6. If antonyms are words that mean the opposite, circle **H**. If not, circle **L**.

7. If a trumpet is a woodwind instrument, circle **Z**. If not, circle **Y**.

8. If Charles Dickens wrote *David Copperfield*, circle **T**. If not, circle **W**.

9. If the Pilgrims landed on Plymouth Rock in 1492, circle **S**. If not, circle **C**.

10. If a telescope is used to view things far away, circle **K**. If not, circle **M**.

11. If the Louvre is located in London, circle **E**. If not, circle **I**.

Service in the Park

Four students from Parktown Middle School are participating in a community service project at Middle Park. The students mow the grass in different parts of the park every day. The four students take turns mowing.

Directions: Solve the word problems and show your work.

1. One of the students has decided to mow the grass on the northern side of the park. The measurements of the northern side of the park are 45.7 meters x 15.2 meters. What is the area of the northern side of the park?	4. A group of volunteers started collecting the leaves on the southern side of the park. They were able to bag 10 sq. meters of leaves in 7 minutes. If they bagged the leaves on the entire south lawn, about how long would it take them to bag the leaves?
2. If he can mow 15 sq. meters of grass in 10 minutes, about how long will it take him to mow 300 sq. meters? (*Hint:* Begin by dividing 300 by 15.)	5. How did you calculate the answer to problem # 4?
3. The measurements of the southern side of the park are 45 meters x 20 meters. What is the area of the southern side of the park?	6. If the students collected 50 bags of leaves from the southern lawn, how many bags of leaves would they probably collect from an area one and a half times the size of the south lawn?

The Zoo of Friendly Living

Part I

Directions: Use this glossary to help you fill in the missing words in the story below.

> **colossal** — huge **inception** — beginning **mustang** — a wild horse
>
> **confound** — to confuse **critters** — creatures **wallow** — to roll in mud

The Zoo of Friendly Living has announced major changes to some of its attractions. Please pick up the information sheet at the zoo's entrance so that the changes will not (1) _____ you. The zoo has expanded the grasslands, so that its prized (2) _____ may gallop. More dirt and water have been added for the wild pigs to (3) _____. Workers have finished building a (4) _____ tower on which the eagles can build their nests, and little cages have been built for the smaller (5) _____, as well. All of these changes mark the (6) _____ of the zoo's new image.

Part II

Directions: Circle the best new word to match each clue.

1. to create something unclear   **colossal** or **confound**
2. how animals play in the mud   **mustang** or **wallow**
3. a cowboy could tame it   **inception** or **mustang**
4. not tiny at all   **colossal** or **wallow**
5. the start of a new plan   **inception** or **critters**
6. they're everywhere   **confound** or **critters**

Part III

Directions: Choose the best answer.

1. What is a glossary?
   a. an alphabetical list of words related to a specific subject
   b. important words and definitions used in a book
   c. a dictionary of words the reader might not know
   d. all of the above

2. How can a glossary help you?
   a. You can use it to find where in a book a particular word is located.
   b. It can give you ideas for writing topics.
   c. Learning the meanings of new words helps you understand what you read.
   d. It can help you summarize what you read.

Powerful Predators

Killer whales are misnamed. Although they are powerful predators, they aren't whales. Killer whales belong to the scientific family *Delphinidae*, which includes dolphins and porpoises. The origins of the misleading name began back in the 18th century. This was when whalers nicknamed these animals "whale killers" after witnessing their fierce and powerful attacks on much larger prey. Over time, the name became reversed, and the animals became known as "killer whales."

Despite the popularity of the name "killer whale," scientists aren't comfortable with it because of its inaccuracy. They prefer the name "orca." "Orca" comes from the creature's scientific name, *Orcinus orca*. As the name "orca" avoids the word "whale," it is a much better fit for the largest member of the dolphin family. In addition, the negative feelings that one gets from the word "killer" are avoided.

Orcas hunt in groups. Their particular hunting method depends on the circumstances and their prey. Around ice, an orca may spy hop (poke its head out of the water and look around). If prey is spotted on an ice floe, the orca signals other members of its pod, or group, and then swims underneath the edge of the floe. Next, it pushes the floe up, forcing the resting animals to slide down into the water where the other pod members are waiting.

Directions: Refer to the passage to answer the questions.

1. Scientists prefer the name "orca" because

   a. orcas are powerful predators.

   b. orcas eat many different kinds of prey.

   c. orcas hunt in groups.

   d. orcas are members of the dolphin family.

2. From the story, one can definitely tell that 18th-century whalers were witness to orcas

   a. hunting.

   b. protecting their calves.

   c. spy hopping to spot prey.

   d. surging out of the water.

3. Write down the steps an orca follows when it catches an animal resting on an ice floe.

   (1) _____

   (2) _____

   (3) Pod members wait at the other end of the floe.

   (4) _____

Show, Don't Tell

Stories hold our interest more when they show action rather than simply telling what happened. Here are three ways you can use the principle of "show, don't tell" in your writing:

> **Use actions that show how the characters feel.**
>
> She sat at the table, staring blankly at her English homework. Finally, she slammed her pencil down and sighed.
>
> **Include the five senses to show the action in the story.**
>
> Her chair creaked as she leaned back. The warm, smoky smell of barbecue wafted in from the neighbor's yard.
>
> **Include dialogue (characters talking to each other).**
>
> "Mom, if you make me do it now, I'm going to miss the whole party! I can do my homework later!" she complained.
>
> "If you actually get started on your homework, you'll be done in no time," responded her mother.

Directions: Think of an event or activity in which you recently participated. Use the prompts below to brainstorm ways of showing what the experience was like. Then, begin your recount.

Ten sensory details:

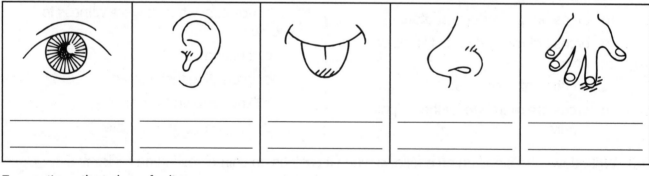

Two actions that show feelings: _____

_____

Three things that people said (or could have said): _____

_____

Begin your recount: _____

_____

_____

Hidden Art

Directions: You will need a copy of page 96 or a piece of graph paper to complete this activity. Look at the chart and write the appropriate number next to each letter. Then use the numbers to fill in the coordinate pairs. On graph paper, plot the points, connecting the dots in the order listed below. A picture will appear.

A = stock value on June 18   A = _____

B = stock value on June 22   B = _____

C = stock value on June 20   C = _____

D = stock value on June 15   D = _____

E = stock value on June 21   E = _____

F = stock value on June 16   F = _____

G = stock value on June 14   G = _____

H = stock value on June 17   H = _____

I = stock value on June 11   I = _____

J = stock value on June 12   J = _____

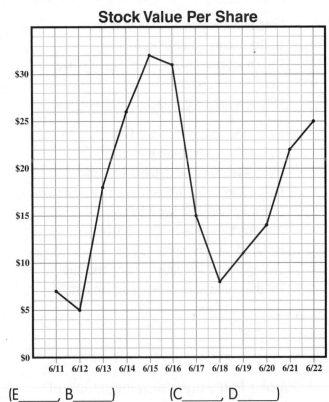

Stock Value Per Share

(B_____, A_____)   (A_____, A_____)   (E_____, B_____)   (C_____, D_____)

(4, A_____)   (A_____, B_____)   (E_____, A_____)   (C_____, F_____)

(J_____, I_____)   END OF LINE   END OF LINE   END OF LINE

(J_____, 2)   (E_____, B_____)   (C_____, D_____)   (H_____, D_____)

(B_____, 2)   (A_____, B_____)   (H_____, D_____)   (H_____, F_____)

(B_____, A_____)   (I_____, G_____)   (17, 34)   END OF LINE

END OF LINE   (I_____, 30)   (17, 36)

                        (A_____, F_____)   (C_____, 39)

(B_____, 6)   (E_____, F_____)   (C_____, 37)

(G_____, 3)   (23, 30)   (12, 34)

(28, J_____)   (23, G_____)   (C_____, D_____)

(28, 10)   (E_____, B_____)   END OF LINE

(G_____, 11)   END OF LINE

(B_____, A_____)

END OF LINE

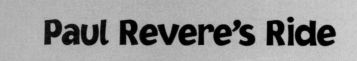

Paul Revere's Ride

Directions: Read the poem excerpt and answer the questions.

Paul Revere's Ride
by Henry Wadsworth Longfellow

1. Listen my children and you shall hear
2. Of the midnight ride of Paul Revere,
3. On the eighteenth of April, in Seventy-five;
4. Hardly a man is now alive
5. Who remembers that famous day and year.

6. He said to his friend, "If the British march
7. By land or sea from town to-night,
8. Hang a lantern aloft in the belfry arch
9. Of the North Church tower as a signal light,—
10. One if by land, and two if by sea;
11. And I on the opposite shore will be,
12. Ready to ride and spread alarm
13. Through every Middlesex village and farm,
14. For the country folk to be up and to arm."

15. Then he said "Good-night!" and with muffled oar
16. Silently rowed to the Charleston shore
17. Just as the moon rose over the bay,
18. Where swinging wide at her moorings lay
19. *The Somerset*, British man-of-war;
20. A phantom ship, with each mast and spar
21. Across the moon like a prison bar,
22. And a huge black hulk, that was magnified
23. By its own reflection in the tide.

24. Meanwhile, his friend through alley and street
25. Wanders and watches, with eager ears,
26. Till in silence around him hears
27. The muster of men at the barrack door,
28. The sound of arms, and the tramp of feet,
29. And the measured tread of the grenadiers,
30. Marching down to their boats on the shore.

1. What is Paul Revere warning people of?
   a. bad weather
   b. a battle
   c. the invasion of the British
   d. a phantom ship

2. If the British attack from sea, how many lanterns will be hung in the North Church?
   a. two
   b. one
   c. three
   d. none

3. Describe what you think happens next in the poem. How does it end?

_____

4. Why might Longfellow admire Paul Revere?

_____

Challenge: Find and read a full version of the poem on the Internet or at the library.

Were your predictions in question three correct? _____

Illuminated Ideas

Renaissance refers to a period of time in Western European history from about the 1300s to the 1600s. The Renaissance is the time that came after the Middle Ages. The word *renaissance* means "rebirth" in French.

What exactly was being reborn during the Renaissance? Basically, there was a renewed interest in the ancient world. There were many factors that caused this renewed interest, one being trade with Eastern Europe. Beginning in Italy, people began to be exposed to ideas that had been lost to Western Europe for a long time. Also, because of increased prosperity, there were more people who could hire artists to create works of art for them, so there were more artists and the arts flourished. Many people also became more interested in the study of antiquity, of Ancient Greek and Roman cultures.

For a long time, the ideas of the Renaissance spread throughout Western Europe mainly through word of mouth. In the mid 1400s, Johannes Gutenberg invented something that would change the world forever. This invention was called the printing press. The printing press made it easier to spread information and ideas.

Prior to the printing press, books were copied and recopied by hand. Because copying a book took such a long time, there weren't that many copies of books around. Many, many people were illiterate. However, when books were rare, sometimes those who could read would share books with those who couldn't. The people who couldn't read developed amazing memories to compensate. The people who wrote out the copies of the books also helped by creating *illuminated letters*. An illuminated letter is the first letter of a passage written large and filled with art that shows what the passage is about.

Directions: Create your own illuminated letter. Choose something you have read recently. It can be anything from a recipe or a magazine article to a chapter of a book. In the space above, write the first letter of the passage and decorate it with art that shows what the passage is about.

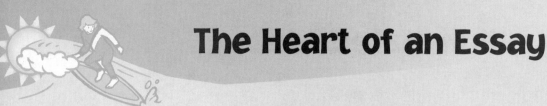

The Heart of an Essay

Most essays are controlled by one central idea. You can think of this as the heart of the essay. This central, or controlling, idea is called the *thesis statement*. A thesis statement must be written in a complete sentence. It is usually found in the last sentence of the introduction.

> my dad's love of swimming
>
> "My dad's love of swimming" is not a complete sentence. There is a topic here but no controlling idea.
>
> If my dad hadn't loved swimming as a teenager, he might not have developed into a landscape designer.
>
> Now we have a topic and a controlling idea. The writer's job now is to explain how her father's love of swimming made him choose landscape designing as his occupation.
>
> ___
>
> I am going to discuss the camera.
>
> Here, once again, we have a topic, but no idea how it will be developed. (Also, if you are going to write an essay about the camera, you do not have to include *I am going to discuss* . . . We already understand this—we have your essay!)
>
> Let's add a controlling idea to our thesis statement.
>
> A camera with a zoom lens will make your pictures more exciting.
>
> Notice that this thesis statement contains a clearly worded opinion—*"Your pictures will be more exciting (with a zoom lens)."*

Directions: Change each thesis statement so that it has one controlling idea.

1. If I had an opportunity to go anywhere in the world, I would choose to see Italy, or perhaps I would go just visit the northern part of my state.

    _____

    _____

    _____

2. The most beautiful season is winter when the snow makes the whole city clean and white, but I like summer when there is no school.

    _____

    _____

    _____

3. Taking care of older family members who need help is a responsibility of everyone, and I well remember how my grandmother told me fascinating stories of her childhood.

    _____

    _____

    _____

Word Problems

Directions: Solve each word problem, showing your work.

1. Trevor's family is moving across country. They will rent a truck to haul their belongings. Behind the truck, they will tow their car. They will drive 2,716 miles. Trevor compares rates from You Do It and Bargain Movers for rental trucks.

You Do It
17' truck
$1,271 for 3,000 miles
Tow package $236.89
10% discount for moves on Mondays

Bargain Movers
16' truck
$1,131 for 2,500 miles
$0.35 per mile over 2,500 miles
Tow package $246.75

   a. What amount would Bargain Movers charge Trevor to move? Show or explain how you got your answer.

   b. Which company offers the best price if Trevor is moving on a Tuesday?

   c. Trevor decides to move on a Monday. Which company would charge him the least amount for his move? Show or explain how you got your answer.

2. You have a lot to do today! You're meeting Micah for lunch at the mall, visiting the science museum, and going to the dentist. Your mom also asked you to take tomatoes from the garden to the neighbor. The mall is closed on Sunday. The science museum is open on Monday, Wednesday, Friday, and Saturday. Your dentist works part time on Thursday and Friday. The neighbor is home only on Friday and Saturday. What day of the week is it today?

3. Brianna played video games three hours less than twice as many hours as Pedro played. Let P represent the number of hours that Pedro played. Write an equation to represent the number of hours that Brianna played.

$$B =$$

Things in Common

Directions: Explain what the items in each list below have in common. Be specific. One has been done for you.

1. beets, carrots, turnips, potatoes _____vegetables that grow underground_____

2. lime, lemon, orange, grapefruit _____

3. plum, peach, pear, pineapple _____

4. September, April, June, November _____

5. cirrus, cumulus, stratus _____

6. tiger, lion, panther, jaguar _____

7. dragons, unicorns, mermaids _____

8. bicycle, train, car, bus _____

9. Texas, Louisiana, Mississippi, Alabama, Florida

_____

10. Maine, Massachusetts, New Jersey, Virginia, South Carolina, Florida

_____

11. California, Arizona, New Mexico, Texas

_____

Roman Numerals in Modern Times

Directions: Use the Roman Numerals key to help you solve the problems.

Roman Numerals									
1	I	2	II	3	III	4	IV	5	V
6	VI	7	VII	8	VIII	9	IX	10	X
50	L	100	C	500	D	1,000	M		

1. Your grandpa's watch has roman numerals on the clock face. The watch is sitting on the bookcase when you walk through the living room. You glance at it to see if it is time to leave for baseball practice yet. What time does the watch show?

2. Your uncle lends you one of his favorite books from middle school to read. Curious, you look to see just how old the book is. What date was this book published?

3. You want to tell your friend your address but you don't want everyone else to know. You decide to use roman numerals to make a secret code for your address. Your address is 417 NE 148th Avenue. What will your address be in roman numerals? (*Hint:* 40 is written as XL.)

Your friend sends back his address using the same code. His address is 1944 NE 52nd Street. How does his address read in roman numerals?

Story Parts

Stories consist of various parts that fit together to form the whole, including the following:

☼ Characters   ☼ Problem   ☼ Actions   ☼ Setting of time   ☼ Setting of place

Directions: Use the chart below to brainstorm ideas for each story part. Examples are included to jumpstart your thinking. Then choose at least one idea from each category and begin a story that incorporates these ideas.

Characters	Setting of Time	Setting of Place	Problem	Action
old woman with white hair and thick glasses	Tuesday (modern day)	neighborhood park	character sees a dog chasing a skunk	hides behind a tree

Start your story: _____

_____

_____

_____

_____

Challenge: Finish your story on a separate sheet of paper.

Cambodia

Directions: Read the article and use the information to solve the crossword puzzle.

Located in the tropics of Southeast Asia, Cambodia is a country that has suffered great political strife and hard times. Yet Cambodia has a rich culture and artistic heritage

The people of Cambodia have developed ways of dealing with the tropical weather. Many houses in Cambodia are built on stilts. This is because Cambodia has a monsoonal climate. Monsoons are winds that change directions twice a year. When the monsoon winds blow across the land to the ocean from November to April, the days are sunny, clear, and dry. But when the monsoon winds change direction, blowing across the ocean toward the land, they carry water. Thus, from May to October, it rains every day, usually for an hour or so in the afternoon. By the end of the rainy season, the soil is saturated.

Cambodia's national language is Khmer. One just can't say "you" in Khmer. Pronouns are used to signify a person's social status, and so the "you" one uses depends on whether one is speaking to a child, a parent, a Buddhist monk, or a member of the royal family.

Livestock production is important in Cambodia because a supply of draft animals is needed. What are draft animals? Draft animals are used for pulling or hauling loads, as well as transportation.

Elephants are also an important part of life in Cambodia. How do the elephants found in Cambodia differ from those found in Africa? Asian (or Indian) elephants have smaller ears. Only the males have tusks. African elephants differ; both the males and females have tusks. Asian elephants are easier to train than African elephants. They are still used today to do heavy work in some parts of southern Asia.

Across

2. A language that has different forms for the pronoun "you" based on a person's social status.

3. Elephants that do heavy work in Cambodia.

6. The way houses in Cambodia are built to avoid flooding (two words).

7. A word for animals used for transportation or to pull or haul loads.

Down

1. Cambodia is located in the _____.

4. The female elephants have tusks.

5. Winds that change direction twice a year.

Alien Activities

Part I

Directions: Find the meaning of each underlined word in the "alien activities" below. Put the letter of the answer on the blank line. Use the definitions in the box below to help you.

> A. artistically attractive
>
> B. foot soldiers
>
> C. a thick stick
>
> D. a steep cliff
>
> E. small hills
>
> F. a message

_____ 1. hang-gliding from a sharp <u>precipice</u> at the North Pole

_____ 2. climbing up and down the moon's gentle <u>hillocks</u>

_____ 3. photographing <u>aesthetic</u> sights in the galaxy

_____ 4. sending a <u>missive</u> to the space station

_____ 5. hunting with a <u>cudgel</u> at the South Pole

_____ 6. marching like <u>infantry</u> on Mars

Part II

Directions: Answer the following questions with your new vocabulary.

1. What is a dangerous spot? _____

2. Where do many flowers grow? _____

3. Who fights battles? _____

4. What is a simple weapon? _____

5. How is information passed? _____

6. What means the same as "lovely"? _____

Challenge: Draw a picture that illustrates as many of these words as you can. Can you illustrate all six words in one picture?

Fun Fractions

Directions: Read the problems carefully and answer the questions. Show your work.

1. Kyaira made trail mix for a hike she will go on with her friends. She used different amounts of several ingredients.

    1 ¼ c. granola

    ¼ c. raisins

    ½ c. peanuts

    1 ¼ c. dried cranberries

    ½ c. chocolate chips

    a. How many cups of trail mix does she have total?

    b. Kyaira will hike with two other friends. If each person has an equal amount of trail mix, how much will each person have?

2. Andrew, Colin, and Jacob will share a new video game system. They will each need to contribute towards the purchase price of $199.98.

    a. How much will each boy need to pay?

    b. Andrew already has $25 saved from mowing lawns over the summer. How much more will Andrew need to save?

3. Mike is buying a new music CD. The price tag says $13.96. There is a sale for ¼ off. A sign advertises that he can buy two CDs for $20.

    a. How much will Mike pay for one CD on sale?

    b. How much money will Mike save?

    c. Which is the better deal, for Mike to buy one CD at ¼ off or to buy two CDs? Explain.

4. Lee and his friends are going to the movies. The theater holds 276 people. When the show starts, only one quarter of the seats will be empty. One third of the people attending will buy popcorn.

    a. How many people will be in the theater at show time?

    b. How many people will buy popcorn?

Sentence Combining

Directions: Revise the following paragraph by combining sentences where appropriate. Use page 103 for correct editing marks. Be sure to read the paragraph out loud. This will help you decide what corrections to make.

When
∧Mrs. Clay was a little girl in the 1960s⸝ $he celebrated her birthdays with her family. She loved parties. Some things about them bothered her. She always thought it was unfair to get too many presents. She knew many children in her community never got anything. Every passing year brought Mrs. Clay more concern. Now Mrs. Clay celebrates her birthdays at a local children's home. She gets some presents. She gives some presents. She thinks this is a meaningful celebration for her family. It shows them that others need their support. Her son, Michael, saves up a part of his allowance all year. He buys gifts for the homeless children. The Clay family is trying to persuade others to have their parties at the children's home. So far they have not been successful.

Brownian Motion

Directions: To do this activity, you will need sunshine, so make sure to do it on a warm day. Read the passage about Brownian motion, then complete the activity below.

> Robert Brown was a Scottish biologist and physicist in the late 1700s and early 1800s. He discovered that when tiny grains of pollen from a plant were placed in a container of water, they never stopped moving. The hotter the water became, the faster the grains of pollen moved. The same phenomenon can be seen in the movement of dust, pollen, and smoke through air. This continual random movement of small particles in air or water is called *Brownian motion*. It was part of the chain of evidence for the existence of atoms and molecules.

1. Find a window with bright sunlight shining through. Look at the sunlight from the side and notice the dust particles in the air. At first they seem stationary, but you will quickly see some of the particles dart about as if hit by invisible forces. They are being moved about by fast-moving, invisible molecules of air. This is Brownian motion.

2. Look for other examples in the air. Check other windows. Look outside along the building. Look for areas of slanting sunlight.

3. Describe what you saw and where you observed examples of Brownian motion.

_____

_____

_____

_____

Challenge: To complete this challenge, you will need some flower pollen or light dust, a magnifying glass, and a small cup of water.

1. Gently drop the pollen or dust into a small cup or container of water.

2. Use a magnifying glass to observe the movement of the pollen or dust on the water.

3. Describe what you see.

_____

_____

_____

_____

Mr. Pythagorean, a city bus driver, told his children Lawrence and Michelle that evening at dinner, "I had a passenger with a conundrum today."

Michelle said, "Is a conundrum some type of large package or something?"

Lawrence answered his little sister's question by explaining, "A conundrum is an exceedingly difficult problem or question where the answer may only be a guess."

Upon hearing the definition of a *conundrum*, Michelle turned to her father and said, "You have piqued my curiosity. What was your passenger's conundrum?"

Mr. Pythagorean explained, "The passenger was a boy who had just bought a fishing rod that was five feet (1.5 m) long. The boy had no other way to get home except by bus, but there's a city ordinance that prohibits anyone carrying packages on the bus longer than four feet (1.2 m)."

"Are you saying that you didn't allow him to board?" demanded Michelle.

"I couldn't let him disobey the rules," Mr. Pythagorean said, "but I found a solution to his conundrum."

"The conundrum being how to get on a bus without breaking the ordinance about the package length with an object longer than what the ordinance allows," said Michelle. "Dad, that's impossible unless he bent the rod, took it apart, or altered it in some other fashion!"

"No, it's not," said Lawrence, grinning. "I know what you had the boy do so he could board the bus with his oversize package and not break the city ordinance."

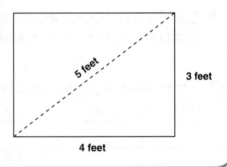

"What?" demanded Michelle.

"You had the boy get a box that was three feet by four feet (.9 by 1.2 m). Then you had the boy place the rod in the box because the diagonal of a three-by-four box is equal to five."

"Exactly!" Mr. Pythagorean said with a smile.

Directions: Answer each question carefully.

1. Which question could be called a conundrum?
   a. Which came first, milk or soda pop?
   b. Which came first, the car or the plane?
   c. Which came first, dogs or cats?
   d. Which came first, the chicken or the egg?

2. Describe a conundrum and a possible solution. Can you think of more than one? Here is an example to get you thinking.

   It is a clear night, and many stars are visible. A son asks his father to point out the North Star. The father says, "That's not possible."

   _____

   _____

   _____

Describing Motion

Any kind of motion can be described by calculating its speed, velocity, and acceleration.

Speed

Speed is a measure of how fast an object moves over a given amount of time. For example, if you travel 200 kilometers in 5 hours, it means that you have traveled at an average speed of 40 kilometers per hour.

To calculate average speed, divide the distance traveled by the time you would need to move that distance. Here is the formula:

$$\text{average speed} = \frac{\text{distance}}{\text{time (hours)}} = 200 \text{ km} \div 5 \text{ h} = 40 \text{ km/h}$$

Let's say that you can ride your bike 5 miles in 20 minutes. To calculate how many miles you could ride in one hour, use the same formula:

Instantaneous speed is the speed of any object at any moment. The speedometer on a car measures instantaneous speed.

Velocity

Velocity is the measurement of the speed and the direction of an object. For example, you may ride your bike 20 mph west to get to the grocery store and then ride back home at 20 mph east.

Acceleration

Acceleration is a measurement of how velocity changes over time. For example, as you ride your bike to the grocery store at a rate of 20 mph west, you may need to apply the brakes at some point during your trip or speed up at other points. These would be examples of acceleration.

Directions: Read each question carefully. Fill in the bubble that corresponds with the best answer.

1. If the speed of a car is 5 miles in 6 minutes (1/10 of an hour), how many miles will it have covered in one hour?
   - ⓐ 55 miles
   - ⓑ 30 miles
   - ⓒ 5 miles
   - ⓓ 50 miles

2. What does velocity measure?
   - ⓐ speed and direction
   - ⓑ speed only
   - ⓒ direction only
   - ⓓ vectors quality

3. Average speed equals
   - ⓐ time divided by distance.
   - ⓑ distance times direction.
   - ⓒ distance multiplied by time.
   - ⓓ distance divided by time.

4. A car traveling at the speed of 10 miles in 15 minutes will travel _____ miles in one hour.

Word Winders

Directions: Use the clues to help you fill in the blanks and boxes. Only the boxed letters change from one word to the next.

	a fish that can be dangerous	s	h	a	r	k
1.	not dull	s	h	a	r	☐
2.	to use together	—	—	—	—	☐
3.	to be concerned	—	☐	—	—	—
4.	a horse-drawn vehicle with two wheels	—	—	—	—	☐
5.	a table with numbers	☐	☐	—	—	—
6.	to delight	—	—	—	—	☐
7.	not soft	—	—	—	☐	
8.	a rabbit	—	—	—	☐	
9.	money paid to ride a bus	—	☐	—	—	
10.	land used to raise crops	—	—	—	☐	
11.	a signal used to give warning	☐	☐	—	—	
12.	a small songbird	—	—	—	☐	
13.	the sound a dog makes	—	☐	—	—	
14.	without light	—	☐	—	—	
15.	to have sufficient courage	—	—	☐		
16.	a fruit	—	—	☐	—	
17.	after the expected time	—	☐	—	—	
18.	in a bowling alley	—	—	☐	—	
19.	a walking stick	☐	—	—		
20.	a wafer for holding ice cream	—	☐	—		
	finished	d	o	n	e	

Bob's Deli

Bob owns a deli. He often has to change recipes to suit the number of people he estimates he will have to serve.

Directions: Complete the input/output tables to change the recipes to serve different numbers of people.

Party Fruit Salad

Rule: _____ Multiply the recipe by three. _____

Serves 8 people	Serves _____ people
6 cups watermelon	
2 cups raisins	
3 apples	
½ cup cherries	
1 lb. strawberries	3 lbs. strawberries
1 mango	

Chili

Rule: _____

Serves 6 people	Serves _____ people
2 lbs. turkey meat	1 lb. turkey meat
8 ounces cooked black beans	
16 ounces cooked kidney beans	
⅓ tsp. fresh garlic	
½ tsp. salt	¼ tsp. salt
⅕ lb. snap beans	
1 package of chili powder	
1 cup salsa	

Vanilla

Directions: Read the passage and use the information to answer the questions.

> Thomas Jefferson is known for many things. He was a founding father and principal author of the Declaration of Independence. He was president from 1801 to 1809. These accomplishments are well known, but Jefferson did something else, too; he introduced a flavor to the newly formed United States.
>
> Vanilla is derived from an orchid. Vanilla is native to the tropical regions of Central America. It is also native to the northernmost regions of South America. Long ago, the Totonac people of Mexico learned to cultivate the vanilla plant. They learned to dry and grind its seed pod so it would release its hidden flavor. The Totonacs used vanilla whenever they prepared a drink we know of today as chocolate.
>
> The Aztecs, also a people of long-ago Mexico, conquered the Totonacs around 1425. Part of the tribute the Aztecs insisted the Totonacs pay was vanilla. Hernán Cortés, a Spanish conqueror, first tasted chocolate and its added vanilla when it was offered to him by the Aztecs in 1519. He brought vanilla seed pods back to Europe to be used in the preparation of chocolate.
>
> Europeans didn't realize vanilla was a delicious flavor in its own right until 1602. The discovery was made by Hugh Morgan. Morgan's job was to prepare herbal medicines for Queen Elizabeth I. Queen Elizabeth adored the taste, and its popularity spread. Jefferson first tasted vanilla when he was the minister to France in 1785. When Jefferson returned home, he carried vanilla pods with him so that he could introduce the flavor to his young country.

1. Which statement is false?
   a. Queen Elizabeth I adored the taste of vanilla.
   b. Vanilla was used to enhance the flavor of chocolate.
   c. People in Mexico first cultivated vanilla.
   d. Jefferson brought back vanilla after he was president.

2. What is true about vanilla? Vanilla is
   a. a flavor native to Europe.
   b. a favorite flavor of Cortés.
   c. a flavor derived from an orchid.
   d. a flavor used only with chocolate.

3. Use information from the passage to fill in the timeline. Use every date mentioned in the story.

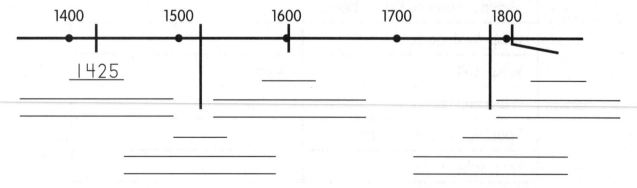

The Amazing Hand

The human hand has five fingers, 14 joints, and 27 bones. You can rotate it 180°. The fingers are controlled by a web of tendons that allows them to do remarkable things such as painting a picture, holding a bat, or writing a story. The most extraordinary part of the hand is the thumb that can touch each of the other four fingertips and can swing around in a circle. This is called the "opposable" thumb and enables humans to grasp and grip objects and to twist and manipulate the hand in ways that no other creature can. This dexterity has helped humans invent the most complex tools and machinery.

Directions: To do these activities, you will need medical or masking tape. You will also need access to common household items. Do all experiments carefully, using good judgment, then write down your observations on this page.

1. Tape your right thumb (or left if you're left-handed) so that it is right next to the palm of your hand and you can't use it. If you are able, repeat with the other thumb. If not, fold your thumb as if it is taped and don't use it during this experiment.

2. Then, choose two or more of the following activities to try based on what materials you have at hand. With your thumb(s) taped:
   - Hold a baseball or tennis ball. Try to bounce the ball off a wall and catch it. Try different ways to hold the ball and grip it.
   - Dribble a basketball or volleyball. Try to shoot the basketball or serve the volleyball.
   - Try to shuffle a deck of cards or deal cards to players.
   - Try to use a pencil eraser or sharpen a pencil.
   - Try to play checkers, chess, or any other game with pieces to move.
   - Type on a computer or use a mouse.
   - Comb your hair and button a shirt or jacket.

3. Try to describe what happened on this page with your thumbs still taped. _____
   _____
   _____

   What did you have to do to write without thumbs? _____
   _____
   _____

4. Take the tape off your thumbs and describe your experiences. _____
   _____
   _____
   _____

Sentence Ingredients

There are many phrases that will help you as you write expository paragraphs and essays. Some are used when we are ordering writing by time or sequence. The following are a few of the most common:

- ✿ **after**—**After 11:00** AM, it is too late to leave for work.
- ✿ **before**—**Before the beginning** of the game, the fans were quiet.
- ✿ **by**—Meet me in front of the museum **by 3:00** PM.
- ✿ **at**—**At noon**, all the restaurants are full.
- ✿ **during**—The crowd was on its feet **during the final seconds**.

Here are more words that place ideas or events in sequential order:

> ✿ **first**   ✿ **then**   ✿ **second**   ✿ **last**   ✿ **next**   ✿ **finally**

Directions: Fill in the blanks in the following paragraph with the appropriate expression of time or sequence from the lists above.

Every fan in town was excited about the annual high school championship football game. _____ one o'clock, everyone was in their seats. _____ the band played "The Star-Spangled Banner" and everyone stood and cheered. _____ our team came out. You could not hear yourself think with all the noise. _____ the game even started, my throat was hurting from screaming. _____ exactly three o'clock, the referee held the football. _____ a little girl wandered out on the field, and everyone got very quiet. _____ about thirty seconds, a policeman came and took the girl into the stands. _____ , the game began.

Now look at more transitional words that can be used to show sequence:

> ✿ **while**   ✿ **when**   ✿ **meanwhile**   ✿ **simultaneously**

Directions: On the lines below, compose three sentences linked together with any combination of these transitions.

_____

_____

_____

_____

_____

Favorite Flavors

Directions: Read the clues and solve the logic puzzle to figure out each person's last name and favorite flavor. Use the process of elimination. When you figure out one correct answer, be sure to eliminate all other choices for that person in that category. Also eliminate all other people from that flavor or last name's row. You will need to go through the clues more than once.

Clues

1. The one who likes vanilla isn't Jose or Emanuel.

2. Henry, whose last name is not West, does not like almond.

3. Mr. Herr loves peppermint.

4. Borris' last name isn't Lasher, and he loves chocolate.

5. Mr. Lasher likes almond.

6. Emanuel doesn't like almond.

7. Jose's last name isn't West or Sposito.

8. Henry's last name begins with an H, and he does not like strawberry.

9. Mr. Murphy's first name isn't Jose, and he also doesn't like strawberry.

10. Mr. Sposito prefers vanilla.

	Jose	Paul	Borris	Emanuel	Henry
Herr					
Sposito					
Lasher					
West					
Murphy					
vanilla					
almond					
peppermint					
chocolate					
strawberry					

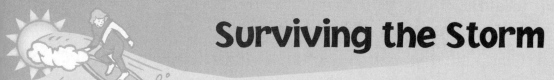

Surviving the Storm

Gabriella and Sarah's progress up the treacherous slopes of K2 was a race with a bank of black clouds. Gabriella and Sarah had planned and trained for the assault on K2, a peak in the Karakorum Range and the second-highest mountain in the world, with great care, but now they were exhausted, oxygen-depleted, and suffering from excruciating hunger.

Although they were at the limit of their physical and mental endurance, they still desired to press on. They knew they were close to the summit, as they were now looking down on surrounding peaks that once towered over them. Numerous climbers had perished on K2, their bodies lost forever on the treacherous slopes, but Gabriella and Sarah believed that they could succeed.

Suddenly, the storm let loose. Instantly, Gabriella and Sarah were blinded, unable to see even their gloved hands in front of their faces. Sharp particles of snow cut their already-frozen faces, and their already-numbed toes and fingers began to freeze. Sarah knew that there was no option but to turn back. She led the way, finding every foothold with her axe alone, for there was no sign of the steps they had painfully cut into the ice on the way up.

It took 17 hours for the two climbers to reach their last camp. There, they had to huddle for four days in a tiny, cramped tent, only leaving it to shovel away the snow that threatened to bury and suffocate them. It took them two more days to descend, their route no longer recognizable due to recent avalanches, and reach the safety of their base camp. Once there, Sarah was asked by another climber, "How'd it go?"

Sarah replied, "I'd say it went well."

"How can you say that?" Gabriella gasped.

"We're alive," Sarah said.

Directions: Read each question and select the best answer.

1. How did Sarah respond to another climber's question?
   a. She said they reached the summit.
   b. She gave a vivid description of their climb.
   c. She understated the difficulties they faced.
   d. She didn't tell the truth.

2. When something is *excruciating*, it is
   a. cold and dangerous.
   b. agonizing and extreme.
   c. powerful and recognizable.
   d. treacherous and suffocating.

3. In the box to the right, draw a rough map of K2, including the following:
   ✿ their base camp
   ✿ the summit
   ✿ their highest camp
   ✿ a recent avalanche area
   ✿ where Sarah and Gabriella might have reached

Native American Words

Today, there are about 2.5 million people who identify themselves as Native American (or American Indian) in the United States and Canada. This number represents about 500 tribes and about 200 different Native American languages. It is believed that in 1492, there were over 500 Native American languages spoken in North America. When you think about these numbers, it is no wonder that many words from Native American languages have been adopted into the English language.

Directions: Draw lines to match each Native American word to its meaning. Begin with words you know and use the process of elimination.

caucus	cooked lima beans and corn
moose	a masked mammal
raccoon	a very large type of deer
hickory	an animal or nature symbol
hominy	dried meat
succotash	a tree with very hard wood
moccasin	ground corn
pemmican	leather footwear
totem	a political meeting

Challenge: In the United States, 26 states have Native American names. How many of these can you name?

_____   _____   _____   _____

_____   _____   _____   _____

_____   _____   _____   _____

_____   _____   _____   _____

_____   _____

Fitting More into Sentences

Writers always want to make their sentences more interesting and informative. One way to do this is to use compound subjects and compound verbs. These terms sound intimidating, but you will understand them easily once you look at a couple of examples.

> A *compound subject* consists of two or more people, places, or things.
>
> Both **Canada and Mexico** border the United States.
>
> A *compound verb* consists of two or more actions.
>
> The children **ran and jumped** all over the new equipment.

Directions: Read each sentence carefully. Identify whether the sentence has a compound subject, compound verb, both a compound subject and compound verb, or neither.

1. The coach and the team were very upset about the loss.

   a. compound subject   c. both

   b. compound verb   d. neither

2. My mother painted and redecorated my bedroom.

   a. compound subject   c. both

   b. compound verb   d. neither

3. The mayor held a conference regarding the proposed tax hike.

   a. compound subject   c. both

   b. compound verb   d. neither

4. The teachers and the students sang and danced at the end-of-the-year fair.

   a. compound subject   c. both

   b. compound verb   d. neither

5. Most people own at least one television set.

   a. compound subject   c. both

   b. compound verb   d. neither

6. The leopards and the lions slept and hid the whole time we were at the zoo.

   a. compound subject   c. both

   b. compound verb   d. neither

7. The puppy barked and whined all night long!

   a. compound subject   c. both

   b. compound verb   d. neither

8. Senators and representatives are all elected by the people of the United States.

   a. compound subject   c. both

   b. compound verb   d. neither

Essay Writing

Directions: Read this student essay about driving and answer the questions that follow.

Middle school students dream of the day they will be able to drive. The freedom of going where you want is very exciting. Of course, parents are nervous about having their children behind the wheel, and there are important considerations concerning safety. However, having a teenager driving relieves the parent of many obligations, helps the teen to learn responsibility, and allows the young driver to understand how to handle problems. There are many significant positive reasons parents should think about that make teenage driving an important experience for maturing.

Parents are so busy in today's world. They must work extra hours to meet their financial commitments. Having a teenage driver will help parents. The teenager can help pick up younger brothers and sisters from school or activities so parents won't have to rush home. The young driver can run errands like getting groceries. In an emergency there will be another driver at home who can help. The teen driver can assist parents with each of these necessities.

Taking care of a car will teach a teen responsibility. First, the teen will need to make sure the car is in good running condition. Second, he or she will learn to understand the importance of safe driving techniques. Finally, a driver must learn the rules of the road, and even a teen who might have been spoiled by thinking only of him- or herself will soon learn to recognize others first.

All drivers face problems, and this will help a teen mature. He or she might get a flat tire and have to deal with that emergency. He or she will have to learn how to find and follow directions. He or she will need to schedule time to arrive on time for appointments. Most importantly, he or she will learn that having privileges always comes with necessary duties. All of these are important adult lessons.

Parents may feel that having a car is too much responsibility for a teenager. However, it is actually a great way to teach responsibility. Parents want to teach their children to become adults they can be proud of. Becoming a careful and concerned driver might be the very best way to acquire these adult qualities.

1. What type of essay is this?
   (a) analytical
   (b) persuasive
   (c) comparison-and-contrast
   (d) narrative

2. What is the thesis statement? _____

_____

3. Which of these is not a supporting point?
   (a) Driving will help a teen mature.
   (b) Having a teenage driver will help parents.
   (c) Parents are so busy in today's world.
   (d) Taking care of a car will teach a teen responsibility.

Hidden Meanings

Directions: Write the phrase shown in each box.

man / board	cycle cycle cycle	COW
1. _____	2. _____	3. _____

K C E H C	TIME AB DE	1,00 **1** 0,000
4. _____	5. _____	6. _____

DECI SION	TOUCH	GI / CCC
7. _____	8. _____	9. _____

Challenge

Directions: Solve each challenge.

Part I

The answer is "a hexagon." Write two questions to which this could be the answer.

_____

_____

_____

_____

Part II

1. How many years are there in a decade? _____

2. How many years are there in a century? _____

3. How many years are there in a millennium? _____

4. When will we enter the next millennium? _____

Part III

1. What do you call the person who mows the grass on a baseball field?

   _____

2. Make up your own riddle involving math terms.

   _____

   _____

Part IV

1. How many dots are there on a die? _____

2. How many degrees are there in a circle? _____

3. Can there be two right angles in a triangle? _____

4. How many degrees are there in a right angle? _____

5. What does the word *perimeter* mean? _____

Using a Hook

As you know, an essay's introductory paragraph gets the reader's attention and introduces the essay's topic. Many people choose to begin their introductions with *hooks*, sentences designed to draw the reader in. A good hook will introduce the topic in a way that gets the reader thinking and makes him or her want to read more.

A hook doesn't need to tell the reader everything about the topic, but it does need to grab the reader's attention. The sentences following the hook finish introducing the topic and giving background information. Then, the final sentence of the introduction states the *thesis*, which is an attitude or central idea.

Part I

Directions: Rewrite these sentences and make them into good hooks. If you get stuck, try beginning your rewrites with words or phrases like:

"Imagine . . ."

"Can you believe . . ."

"Five years from now . . ."

1. Almost all students look forward to summer vacation. _____

_____

2. Eating often at fast-food restaurants can cause health problems. _____

_____

3. Computer training is important for the future. _____

_____

Part II

Directions: Choose one hook and write it below. Then, write the rest of the introductory paragraph. Remember, the introductory paragraph should give information about the topic and state the thesis.

_____

_____

_____

_____

_____

_____

_____

_____

_____

Fun in the Colonies

Although they valued opportunities to have fun, every member of the family and the colonial community worked long hours. Children arose at dawn with the rest of the family. They gathered firewood, shucked corn, ran errands, fed the animals, milked cows, worked in the garden, cut wood, made brooms, churned butter, made candles and soap, and often helped prepare meals or clean up afterward.

When they were not doing chores, children enjoyed many simple games and activities. They liked walking on stilts, rolling hoops, or playing with tops. They played hide-and-seek. Children made and flew kites and went fishing in nearby brooks. They also had swings on trees and seesaw boards. They bowled on grass or dirt, and rolled marbles. Some colonists also enjoyed playing board games, charades, card games, and chess in the evening. A few had time to read or play a musical instrument, such as the violin.

Blind Man's Bluff

This game is a little like tag. It must be played in a clear, open area because the person who is "it" is blindfolded. The other players try to move quietly and avoid getting tagged. Sometimes, after tagging a player, the "it" person must figure out who he or she has tagged by touching the other person's face.

Quoits

This game is very similar to horseshoes. Players have rings that they must throw at a spike. Sometimes the goal is to throw the ring over the spike as it sticks out of the ground, and sometimes, the spike just marks the target area. Over the years, people created many variations. In fact, it is possible you have played quoits if you have been to a fair. Fair attendees may visit booths where they try to throw a ring over a prize. If they succeed, they can keep the prize.

Directions: Compare/contrast the information here with children's lives today. Fill out the chart, keeping in mind what chores you had and what you did for fun as a kid.

Colonial Times	Things in Common	Modern Day

Rat's Discussion

Rat's Discussion of the River Community
from *The Wind in the Willows* by Kenneth Grahame

"But isn't it a bit dull at times?" the Mole ventured to ask. "Just you and the river, and no one else to pass a word with?"

"No one else to—well, I mustn't be hard on you," said the Rat with forbearance. "You're new to it, and of course you don't know. The bank is so crowded nowadays that many people are moving away altogether: O no, it isn't what it used to be, at all. Otters, kingfishers, dabchicks, moorhens, all of them about all day long and always wanting you to do something—as if a fellow had no business of his own to attend to!"

"What lies over there?" asked the Mole, waving a paw towards a background of woodland that darkly framed the water-meadows on one side of the river.

"That? O, that's just the Wild Wood," said the Rat shortly. "We don't go there very much, we river-bankers."

"Aren't they—aren't they very nice people in there?" said the Mole, a trifle nervously.

"W-e-ll," replied the Rat, "let me see. The squirrels are all right. And the rabbits—some of 'em, but rabbits are a mixed lot. And then there's Badger, of course. He lives right in the heart of it; wouldn't live anywhere else, either, if you paid him to do it. Dear old Badger! Nobody interferes with him. They'd better not," he added significantly.

"Why, who should interfere with him?" asked the Mole.

"Well, of course—there—are others," explained the Rat in a hesitating sort of way.

Directions: Use the graphic organizer to compare Rat's observations of those who populate his community to your observations of your community. What traits do you notice in the characters in this excerpt? How are they similar to or different from the character traits of people you know? The chart has been started for you.

River Community Traits	Similarities/Differences in My Community
crowded	
diverse	
Badger would never want to move.	

From Graph to Picture

Directions: Solve each word problem. Use the answers to complete the ordered pairs. Make a copy of page 96 or use your own graph paper to plot the points on paper. Connect the points in the order shown. They will form a picture.

This week Tom worked for 1,140 minutes. **A** is the number of hours that Tom worked.	A = _____
A bicyclist travels 6.5 miles in a half hour. **B** is the number of miles the bicyclist travels in one hour.	B = _____
Kim started to nap at 1:15 P.M. and woke at 1:44 P.M. **C** is the number of minutes she napped.	C = _____
A train goes 25 miles per hour. **D** is the number of hours it needs to go 125 miles.	D = _____
A limousine gets 8 miles per gallon of gas. **E** is the number of miles it can go on 3 gallons.	E = _____
A cheetah runs 11 meters per second. **F** is the number of meters it runs in 2 seconds.	F = _____
A triangle has interior angles of 87°, 66°, and **G**°.	G = _____
A bus goes 400 miles on 25 gallons of gas. **H** is the bus's miles per gallon.	H = _____
A wheel with a circumference of 3 inches is rotating at 5 rotations per minute. **I** is the distance the wheel travels in one minute.	I = _____
A 4-sided shape has interior angles of 71°, 200°, 77°, and **J**°.	J = _____

(I_____, G_____)	(H_____, E_____)	(A_____, 31)	(B_____, J_____)
(C_____, G_____)	(H_____, 39)	(23, G_____)	(I_____, J_____)
(C_____, E_____)	(A_____, 39)	END OF LINE	(I_____, 9)
(A_____, E_____)	(A_____, C_____)	(23, E_____)	(B_____, 9)
(18, 26)	(17, 28)	(25, D_____)	(B_____, J_____)
(4, 26)	(17, B_____)	END OF LINE	END OF LINE
(4, C_____)	(14, B_____)	(4, D_____)	(18, D_____)
(14, C_____)	(14, 23)	(30, D_____)	(18, B_____)
(I_____, G_____)	(H_____, E_____)	END OF LINE	(F_____, B_____)
END OF LINE	END OF LINE	(A_____, F_____)	(F_____, D_____)
	(9, D_____)	(21, F_____)	END OF LINE
	(11, 26)	(21, A_____)	(A_____, 10)
	END OF LINE	(A_____, A_____)	(A_____, 9)
	(J_____, C_____)	(A_____, F_____)	END OF LINE
	(H_____, 32)	END OF LINE	
	END OF LINE		

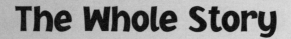

The Whole Story

A complete story has a beginning, a middle, and an end. The beginning introduces the characters and the problem. In the middle of the story, the characters react to the situation and/or do some things to try to solve the problem. At the end, the characters solve the problem, and the story concludes.

Directions: Use the chart and questions below to think of a beginning, middle, and end for a story. If you need help getting started, use characters and a problem or challenge from the box.

three elderly men	a diamond thief	a gossiping high school student
a super-intelligent bird	a sports celebrity	no way to get to an important event
a ruined reputation	witnessing a crime	wanting to stop an injustice
wanting to solve a mystery		trying to save someone from physical danger

Beginning

How does the story start?

Who is involved?

What is the problem?

Middle

How do the characters react in the situation?

What do they do?

How do the characters try to solve the problem?

End

How does the story end?

How is the problem resolved?

How do the characters overcome any obstacles?

Compounds

An *element* is a pure substance that is formed from only one type of atom. For example, oxygen is an element because it is made only of oxygen atoms.

But Earth is full of many other kinds of materials that are combinations of more than one type of atom. For example, when hydrogen and oxygen atoms come together in just the right quantities, water is produced. Water is not an element, it is a compound.

A *compound* is a substance that is produced from the bonding of two or more elements. In any chemical compound, every tiny particle of the substance has the exact ratio of elements as every other tiny particle in the substance. Water is produced when two hydrogen atoms and one oxygen atom bond. That means that every drop of water, no matter where it is, has a ratio of two hydrogen atoms to one oxygen atom.

Directions: Answer the questions and complete the chart.

1. What is an element made of? _____

2. What is a compound made of? _____

3. How many of the following elements can you find in your household? Look at ingredient lists on food and household products. Check each element you find and write the product in which it is found. An example has been completed for you.

Element or Compound		Product
sodium	√	crackers
magnesium		
calcium		
iron		
iodine		

Challenge: What additional elements can you find?

Element or Compound		Product
gold		
tin		
copper		
chlorine		
carbon		

Where Did Spider-Man Come From?

Directions: Read the passage and answer the questions.

Just one man created many of the comic-book heroes we are familiar with today. This celebrated comic-book author's name is Stan Lee. Lee's real name was "Stanley Leiber," but his byline is "Stan Lee."

Readers considered Lee's comics to be fun, entertaining, thrilling, and imaginative, and they loved his innovative characters. Among Lee's new and changed characters were Mr. Fantastic, the Invisible Girl, the Human Torch, and the Thing (all of the Fantastic Four). Lee also created the Incredible Hulk, the Mighty Thor, Iron Man, Doctor Strange, Daredevil, and the X-Men.

Perhaps Lee's most famous character is Spider-Man. Lee said he was trying to think of an innovative and unique superpower for a superhero, but he was having trouble because there were already characters that were the strongest in the world, could fly, could turn invisible, etc. In the midst of his musings, Lee spotted a fly on the wall. Watching the fly led Lee to think about a superhero whose unique superpower could be the power to stick on a wall like an insect. Lee first thought of Mosquito-Man for a name, but he decided against it because it didn't have any glamour. He thought of Insect-Man, but he decided that was even worse. After running through several more names, Lee came up with a name that he felt sounded mysterious and dramatic—Spider-Man.

1. Write down the first two adjectives, thoughts, or images that come to mind when you read the following names:

   Mosquito-Man _____ _____

   Insect-Man _____ _____

   Fly-Man _____ _____

   Lizard-Man _____ _____

   Spider-Man _____ _____

2. If you could be an existing superhero or have a special kind of superpower, who would you be or what power would you have? Write one paragraph explaining your answer.

   _____

   _____

   _____

   _____

   _____

Show Your Work

Directions: Solve the problems. Show how you got your answers using words, numbers, and/or pictures. Fill in the bubbles that correspond with the correct answers.

1. The Venn diagram below shows the number of boys in Ezana's neighborhood who play soccer, play baseball, play both soccer and baseball, or play neither. What is the total number of boys who do not play soccer?

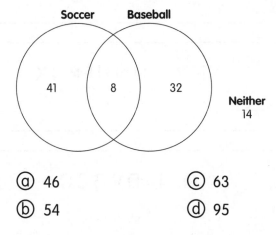

Soccer   Baseball

41   8   32

Neither
14

   (a) 46   (c) 63

   (b) 54   (d) 95

2. Ticket lines are long at Fisher Auditorium. Rocks 'n Raps, one of the most popular groups ever, is giving a concert on Saturday. The tickets went on sale at the beginning of the week. Fifteen hundred tickets were sold on Monday. On Tuesday, 1,800 tickets were sold. If sales continue to increase at this rate, how many tickets will be sold on Saturday?

   (a) 3,700   (c) 3,000

   (b) 1,350   (d) 2,000

3. Irina is riding in a bicycle race. Two-thirds of the course runs uphill. One-third runs downhill. When Irina rides uphill, she rides at an average speed of 8 miles per hour. When she rides downhill, she rides at an average speed of 16 miles per hour. If the course measures 60 miles total how long does it take Irina to finish the race? (*Hint:* Divide the number of miles by the miles per hour.)

   (a) 32 hours   (c) 5.55 hours

   (b) 6.25 hours   (d) 6.45 hours

Author Puzzle

Directions: Below is a list of author names in code. Each letter represents a different letter. The same code is used throughout. Brainstorm some names that could be on the list and look for them by counting letters. As you go, use the known letters to help you decode other names.

1. NJG <u>A V I</u>	7. ZP. RQHRR _____
2. AHZK IFHEQ _____	8. YNPK UNHFRQX _____
3. P. F. RCGXQ _____	9. Q. I. DVGCQ _____
4. IQJQPFK SFQNPK _____	10. A. P. P. CWFTGQX _____
5. PWNFZ ZNVF _____	11. ENPT CDNGX _____
6. A. T. PWDFGXY _____	12. FWGR FWDPK _____

Challenge: Use the code to write the name of your favorite author.

Metric Fun

Directions: Find solutions to these problems and test your knowledge of measurement. If needed, you can refer to Measurement Tools on page 104.

1. What temperature Celsius would be great snow skiing weather?

   a. 23° C

   b. -4° C

   c. −20° C

   d. 32° C

2. You have 250 ml of juice. What type of container do you probably have?

   a. drinking cup

   b. water bottle

   c. jug

   d. test tube

3. What is the width of an average doorway?

   a. 1 yd.

   b. 24 in.

   c. 80 cm

   d. 2 m

4. You can walk 3 mph. How many km will you travel in an hour?

   a. 4.2 km

   b. 4 km

   c. 4.8 km

   d. 5 km

5. About how long is a pen?

   a. 14 km

   b. 14 mm

   c. 14 in.

   d. 14 cm

Challenge: Come up with a measurement problem of your own, using page 104 for reference. Come up with four possible answers, then try your problem out on a friend or family member.

_____

_____

a. _____   c. _____

b. _____   d. _____

A Preposterous Tale

A selfish king in Thailand once announced a contest. To receive a large lump of gold and the hand of the king's daughter in marriage, a man would only have to tell a story that was a lie, the verdict resting on the king's four counselors. This might seem an easy task, but no matter how preposterous the story was, the four counselors would always say, "Yes, this story could be true."

One day a simple farmer arrived at the court, stood before the king, and said, "Long, long ago, a boy tried to catch five elephants so he could ride them. The elephants fled from the boy, and the boy gave chase. He chased the magnificent creatures over mountains, rivers, lakes, and fields. As preposterous as it sounds, he even chased them up trees and across the ocean bottom! Somehow, whenever the boy came close, the elephants managed to escape.

"All this chasing took time, and the boy grew to be an elderly man who could no longer walk. The elderly man asked his son to continue the chase. I am that elderly man's son, now grown, and I caught the elephants a few years past. When I caught the elephants, I rode them into this very city, where I met four very wise counselors, the very four who will issue the verdict on my story today!

"Those four counselors were so impressed by my magnificent elephants that they wanted to purchase them. The price of the elephants was so high that the counselors promised to pay me at a later date. The date they agreed to is today. If the counselors and king agree that my story is true, please pay the money you owe to me. If it's false, bring out my reward and the princess!"

Directions: Look back at the passage to answer the questions.

1. When something is preposterous, it is
   a. so clearly wrong it is laughable.
   b. so impressive it deserves a reward.
   c. so great it is simply magnificent.
   d. so expensive it cannot be paid immediately.

2. From the story, one can tell that most likely
   a. elephants run very fast.
   b. Thailand has or once had a king.
   c. only a king could ride on an elephant.
   d. it is very hard to catch elephants.

3. Fill in the chart with information about the elements from the story, "A Preposterous Tale."

Setting	
Characters	
Problem	
Action	farmer tells story about selling elephants to counselors
Likely Result	

Rock and Roll

The study of how rocks are formed is called geology. There are three basic types of rocks:

Igneous Rock

Igneous rocks are the source material for all three rocks. They start out as liquid magma deep in the Earth. This liquid rock flows to the surface as lava during volcanic eruptions and then hardens.

> **Characteristics**
> ✿ The surfaces can be glossy or porous.
> ✿ Many rocks include crystals that twinkle.
> ✿ A few are light enough to float on water.

Sedimentary Rock

The gradual breakdown of rock by erosion creates particles of rock. Sedimentary rock is formed when particles of rock, sand, seashells, pebbles, and plant material wash into the oceans and sink to the ocean floor. This sediment forms layers that gradually harden under the weight of the water and the accumulated weight of other layers of sediment forming on top.

> **Characteristics**
> ✿ There are lines and layers in the stone.
> ✿ They are often softer than other rocks.
> ✿ The rocks often contain a mix of large and small pieces.

Metamorphic Rock

Metamorphic rock is formed when igneous rock or sedimentary rock is subjected to both heat and pressure. Most metamorphic rock is formed deep within Earth's crust. Sometimes one type of metamorphic rock is changed to another kind by continued heat and pressure.

> **Characteristics**
> ✿ Some have layers of crystals.
> ✿ These rocks are usually very hard.
> ✿ There may be twisted bands of dark and light minerals.

Directions: Determine which type each rock below belongs to, and mark it with an **I**, **S**, or **M**.

_____ Obsidian is often glossy and black.

_____ Mudstone is so soft it can be broken with your bare hands.

_____ Sandstone is formed out of small grains of rock and sand.

_____ Quartzite is formed from sandstone.

_____ Pumice can float on water.

_____ Marble is a hard rock formed from limestone.

_____ Granite is formed when magma cools slowly deep in the Earth's crust.

_____ Rock salt is formed when layers of sea salts and minerals harden into rock.

Great Examples

A good expository paragraph will state the topic and controlling idea in the first sentence. There will be examples to support the topic in the middle sentences. The last sentence of the paragraph will conclude the short discussion.

> Going to surf camp is expensive. First, you have to pay for the instruction from qualified teachers who have lifesaving experience. Second, there is the equipment. You'll need a surfboard, of course, but also a wet suit and ocean shoes. Last, you will need transportation to the ocean, which, if you live very far from the water, will require air or train tickets. Just learning to surf might seem easy, but getting ready to learn will cost a great deal of money.

Let's analyze the paragraph.

- ☼ **Topic**—surf camp
- ☼ **Controlling Idea**—is expensive
- ☼ **Support**—cost of instruction, surfboard, wet suit, transportation
- ☼ **Conclusion**—this simple-looking activity will cost a lot

In order to write a good expository paragraph, you need to know the structure and components listed above, and you also need strong supporting examples.

Directions: For each of the following sentences, underline the topic, circle the controlling idea, and jot down two to three examples to support the idea. (If you disagree with the idea, you may rewrite it.)

1. _____ is a good friend since I can always depend on her/him.

   _____

   _____

   _____

2. The mall is a great place to spend the day with your friends.

   _____

   _____

   _____

3. Exercise is an important part of living a healthy life.

   _____

   _____

   _____

Sam's Market

Sam is the manager of the local market. He orders materials for the market based on expected sales. He writes simple equations for the supplies that he will order and the amount of money that the market will make during a particular period of time. When he writes the equations, he uses **x** as a placeholder for the unknown amount.

Directions: Write and solve an equation based on the information in each word problem.

1. Six-month sales (January–June) at the market totaled $72,450. February and March sales were the same amount—$12,250 each month. April sales were $10,000. May sales were $14,500 and June sales were even higher. In June, the sales totaled $16,000. Let x equal the January sales. Write an equation to find the January sales totals. Solve the equation.

2. The sales for the second six months were $76,000. July sales were $12,480. August and September sales each totaled $10,000. October sales were $15,500, which was only $500 less than November. Let x equal the December sales. Write an equation to find the December sales totals. Solve the equation.

3. Sam estimated that for every $20 of groceries sold, the market has to use one paper bag. Let x equal the number of bags that the market will have to use for the entire year. Use the six-month totals from the first two problems and write an equation to find out about how many bags were used last year. Solve the equation.

Riddles

Part I

Directions: Find the meaning of each underlined word in the riddles below. Put the letter of the answer on the blank line.

> A. to gallop   B. to twist together   C. population
> D. held in prison   E. very important   F. tree-lined street

_____ 1. Criminals used to be <u>incarcerated</u> on this famous island in the San Francisco Bay.

_____ 2. The Amazon Rainforest, mostly in this country, has millions of vines, branches, and stems that <u>entwine</u> as they grow.

_____ 3. In Chicago, you can take a drive on a beautiful <u>boulevard</u> that follows the shore of this famous lake.

_____ 4. It was a <u>momentous</u> day when President Kennedy was buried in this cemetery.

_____ 5. This small but strong breed of pony was imported from a <u>populous</u> of ponies on this island.

_____ 6. Wild horses used to <u>lope</u> freely across this Asian desert.

Challenge: See how many of the riddles above you can solve.

Part II

Directions: Draw a line to match each idea with the correct new word.

the opposite of "untangle"	**populous**
cities more so than towns	**boulevard**
the opposite of "unremarkable"	**lope**
faster than a jog	**incarcerated**
smoother than a trail	**entwine**
the opposite of being free	**momentous**

Challenge: Choose one of the new words and try writing your own riddle below. Then give it to a friend to solve.

Up From Slavery

Directions: Read the excerpt and answer the questions carefully.

An Excerpt from *Up From Slavery*

By Booker T. Washington

I was born a slave on a plantation in Franklin County, Virginia. I am not quite sure of the exact place or exact date of my birth, but at any rate I suspect I must have been born somewhere and at some time. As nearly as I have been able to learn, I was born near a crossroads post-office called Hale's Ford, and the year was 1858 or 1859. I do not know the month or the day. The earliest impressions I can now recall are of the plantation and the slave quarters—the latter being the part of the plantation where the slaves had their cabins.

My life had its beginning in the midst of the most miserable, desolate, and discouraging surroundings. This was so, however, not because my owners were especially cruel, for they were not, as compared with many others. I was born in a typical log cabin, about fourteen by sixteen feet square. In this cabin I lived with my mother and a brother and sister till after the Civil War, when we were all declared free.

Of my ancestry I know almost nothing. In the slave quarters and then later I heard whispered conversations among the colored people of the tortures which the slaves including, no doubt, my ancestors on my mother's side, suffered in the middle passage of the slave ship while being conveyed from Africa to America. I have been unsuccessful in securing any information that would throw any accurate light upon the history of my family beyond my mother. She, I remember, had a half-brother and a half-sister. In the days of slavery not very much attention was given to family history and family records—this is, black family records. My mother, I suppose, attracted the attention of a purchaser who was afterward my owner and hers. Her addition to the slave family attracted about as much attention as the purchase of a new horse or cow. Of my father I know even less than of my mother. I do not even know his name. I have heard reports to the effect that he was a white man who lived on one of the nearby plantations. Whoever he was, I never heard of his taking the least interest in me or providing in any way for my rearing. But I do not find especial fault with him. He was simply another unfortunate victim of the institution which the Nation unhappily had engrafted upon it all that time.

1. Why does Booker T. Washington not know the day on which he was born?
   a. He forgot.
   b. Records of slaves were not kept.
   c. It was illegal for slaves to know their birthdays.
   d. Nineteenth-century people never knew their birthdays.

2. Why does Washington refer to his father as "another unfortunate victim of the institution"?
   a. His father was also a slave.
   b. His father, while not a slave, had been conditioned to think that slaves were less than human.
   c. His father had been institutionalized.
   d. His father was a horrible person.

Challenge: In *Up From Slavery*, Washington goes on to describe his adult life, which included many accomplishments that made a difference in the lives of others. Imagine that some day, you will write your autobiography. What accomplishments do you hope to achieve? Write a short passage from your future autobiography that describes one accomplishment as if you have already achieved it.

Plotting a Story

Have you ever watched a movie and felt that it was almost exactly like another movie you had seen? Perhaps only the details seemed different? Think about your favorite movies and/or classic stories. Common plots and/or themes that have been identified include the "Cinderella" type—a person perceived to be of no value actually being of great value. They also include a quest, coming of age, love conquers, thwarted love, etc.

Directions: Choose one movie or book that you know well, and ask yourself the following questions:

- What types of characters are in the story? Are any characters always perfect or completely evil?
- What are the patterns in the story?
- What does the main character want? What problems or challenges does he or she encounter?
- Who helps or hinders the main character along the way?
- Is there any danger?
- What role does the antagonist play?
- How does the character overcome the difficulty?
- How does the story end? Does the hero or heroine reach the desired goal?

Now fill out as much of the following plot chart as you can with information from that story.

The main character (hero) starts out in his or her own ordinary world.	
The hero is presented with a problem and has to leave his or her comfort zone.	
Someone (or something) comes along to help the hero, perhaps giving tools or advice.	
The hero sets out or begins to try harder.	
The hero faces various tests and obstacles, which grow increasingly difficult.	
The hero struggles and seems to be running out of options.	
The hero finally manages to solve the problem.	
The hero deals with consequences of events and may face one last challenge.	
The hero returns to his or her own world with the prize or knowledge won on the quest.	

Challenge: Go through the plot chart again, this time with your own characters and story. Write your information on a separate paper. Now you have a story board, an outline for a story. There are many ways you can write this story: as a comic book, a picture book, a play, a traditional narrative, etc. Choose a format and write your story.

Reading Comprehension

An Excerpt from *The Monkey's Paw*

By W. W. Jacobs

"What was that you started telling me the other day about a monkey's paw or something, Morris?"

"Nothing," said the soldier hastily. "Leastways, nothing worth hearing."

"Monkey's paw?" said Mrs. White curiously.

"Well, it's just a bit of what you might call magic, perhaps," said the sergeant-major offhandedly.

His three listeners leaned forward eagerly. The visitor absent-mindedly put his empty glass to his lips and then set it down again. His host filled it for him.

"To look at," said the sergeant-major, fumbling in his pocket, "it's just an ordinary little paw, dried to a mummy."

He took something out of his pocket and proffered it. Mrs. White drew back with a grimace, but her son, taking it, examined it curiously.

"And what is there special about it?" inquired Mr. White, as he took it from his son and, having examined it, placed it upon the table.

"It had a spell put on it by an old fakir," said the sergeant-major, "a very holy man. He wanted to show that fate ruled people's lives, and that those who interfered with it did so to their sorrow. He put a spell on it so that three separate men could each have three wishes from it." His manner was so impressive that his hearers were conscious that their light laughter jarred somewhat.

"Well, why don't you have three, sir?" said Herbert White cleverly.

The soldier regarded him in the way that middle age is wont to regard presumptuous youth. "I have," he said quietly, and his blotchy face whitened.

"And did you really have the three wishes granted?" asked Mrs. White.

"I did," said the sergeant-major, and his glass tapped against his strong teeth.

"And has anybody else wished?" inquired the old lady.

"The first man had his three wishes, yes," was the reply. "I don't know what the first two were, but the third was for death. That's how I got the paw."

Directions: After reading the passage, select the best answer to each question. Fill in the bubble.

1. Why did the fakir put a spell on the monkey's paw?
   - ⓐ He was vindictive.
   - ⓑ He wanted to show that fate ruled people's lives.
   - ⓒ He had a strange sense of humor.
   - ⓓ It was his job.

2. Of what did the spell consist?
   - ⓐ One man got three wishes.
   - ⓑ Three men got one wish.
   - ⓒ Three men got three wishes each.
   - ⓓ Whoever possessed the paw could wish as long as he had the paw.

3. The passage tells the wish of one person. What is this wish?
   - ⓐ the wish for death
   - ⓑ the wish for money
   - ⓒ the wish for fame
   - ⓓ none of these

4. What is fate?
   - ⓐ the idea that the things that happen to people are predetermined
   - ⓑ the idea that everything is random
   - ⓒ the idea that things are both destined and random
   - ⓓ the idea that chaos rules the world

Mind Benders

Part I

Directions: Using the clues, add two words to make a third word. The first one has been done for you.

1. the nearest star + an antonym of wet = an adjective meaning several

   _____ sun + dry = sundry _____

2. a lightweight bed of canvas + 2,000 lbs. = a type of fabric

   _____

3. a small, green vegetable + food with a shell = something traditionally eaten at baseball games

   _____

4. a large body of water + a male child = a period of time

   _____

Part II

Directions: Create an Alphabetical Orange Menu by filling in as many orange foods as you can think of.

A _____   J _____   S _____

B _____   K _____   T _____

C _____   L _____   U _____

D _____   M _____   V _____

E _____   N _____   W _____

F _____   O _____   X _____

G _____   P _____   Y _____

H _____   Q _____   Z _____

I _____   R _____

Part III

Directions: Answer the question creatively: What if you were born old and grew young? How would your life as a teenager be different?

_____

_____

_____

_____

_____

_____

Triangle Experiment

The ancient Greeks made important discoveries and developed many mathematical theories that are still used today. One of these ancient Greek mathematicians was called Pythagoras. He was the first person to describe Earth as being spherical (round). He also developed theories regarding the connection between math and music. The students of Pythagoras went on to develop the Pythagorean Theorem used with right triangles: $A^2 + B^2 = C^2$

Directions: Cut out the centimeter ruler at the bottom of the page. Use it to measure each side of the triangle. Use the lengths to make $A^2 + B^2 = C^2$ true. When you figure out where each number fits into the equation, write the corresponding letter in the space by that side of the triangle.

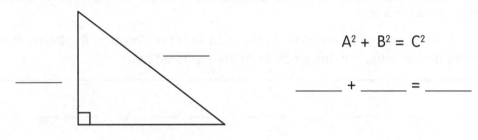

$$A^2 + B^2 = C^2$$

$$\underline{\hspace{1cm}} + \underline{\hspace{1cm}} = \underline{\hspace{1cm}}$$

Challenge: In the space below, create another triangle with lengths that fit the equation. What do these two triangles have in common?

Centimeter Ruler

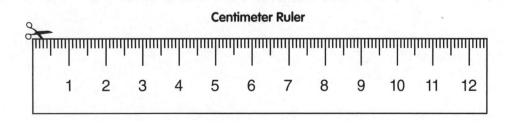

What If?

Directions: Read the story starters below. Choose one and write the rest of the first paragraph. Be creative.

Challenge: Finish your story on a separate piece of paper. Use vivid descriptions.

Story Starter 1: Silently, I walked up to the edge of the crowd. The people were intent, watching some activity on the lakeshore. I stood on my toes and tried to see over the heads of those standing in front of me . . .

Story Starter 2: Once, very long ago, an old woman lived in the remains of a castle. She could not speak, but those who lived in the countryside around knew of her helpfulness . . .

Story Starter 3: Jamal lay in bed staring at the water stain on the ceiling right over his head. The stain was oddly shaped, and he often imagined that it was the outline of a face, trying to tell him something important . . .

Story Starter 4: "Look!" Kira pointed a finger at the light flickering through the trees. It was the middle of the night and they were miles away from the nearest town . . .

_____

_____

_____

_____

_____

_____

_____

_____

_____

_____

_____

Morse Code

Three American inventors used electricity to transform human communications for all time. They created the telegraph, the telephone, and other things that we use today. These advances in electricity then spurred the extraordinary inventions of the 20th and 21st centuries.

Samuel Morse designed his own telegraph. He also created Morse code to make messages clear and simple. It became the most important communication tool of its time. Many other inventors would make improvements on the process for more than 50 years.

Joseph Henry worked in electromagnetism. He developed special magnets essential to Morse's telegraph and provided Morse with a lot of technical help. Henry designed the battery-powered booster relays and insulators for the telegraph lines.

Alexander Graham Bell experimented with a harmonic telegraph, which he hoped would help deaf people hear. As he worked, he began to see that it would be possible to transmit actual speech. In 1876, Bell filed for a patent on the telephone a few hours before another inventor, Elisha Gray, filed a patent on a similar device.

Using Morse Code

Messages are sent in Morse code using only "dots" and "dashes" combined to represent letters. You send a dot by briefly touching the telegraph. A "dash" is held a little longer.

A	G	M	S	Y	4
·—	——·	——	···	—·——	····—
B	H	N	T	Z	5
—···	····	—·	—	——··	·····
C	I	O	U	0	6
—·—·	··	———	··—	—————	—····
D	J	P	V	1	7
—··	·———	·——·	···—	·————	——···
E	K	Q	W	2	8
·	—·—	——·—	·——	··———	———··
F	L	R	X	3	9
··—·	·—··	·—·	—··—	···——	————·

Directions: Use the Morse code shown to convert your name and other words into code. Then, translate the code below to find the word.

cat ———— —·—· ·— —

your full name _____

your birthday _____

the year you were born _____

·· —· ···— · —· — ·· ——— —· ···

_____

Challenge: Write a message to a friend or family member. Then ask him or her to decode it.

Scorpion Studies

Gary Polis knelt down one dark night in a desert sand dune in Southern California. He felt something soft and squishy under his knee. Polis, a biologist, was studying scorpions in their natural habitat. Scorpions are most active at night, but Polis was able to conduct his research using ultraviolet (UV) light. Scorpions glow under UV light, but it doesn't harm or bother them. Scorpion eyes are most sensitive to low levels of light, and scorpions can navigate using shadows cast by starlight.

Knowing that anything soft and squishy was most likely a sidewinder rattlesnake, Polis jumped back immediately. Sidewinders, like all rattlesnakes, are venomous vipers. Unlike scorpions, rattlesnakes do not glow under UV light. Although Polis was not bitten by the snake, he did not escape from harm. When Polis jumped back, he landed on a cactus and ended up with 38 cactus spines in his backside.

To prevent further injury from surprise snake encounters, Polis did two things. First, he caught some of the rattlesnakes in the vicinity and sprayed them with paint that glowed under UV light. Second, he began to wear special snake chaps that were made of woven brass metal.

Over the years, Polis has studied many different species of scorpions around the world. (There are about 1,500 known scorpion species, with only about 25 species venomous enough to kill a human.) One scorpion Polis studied ended up being a record holder. The scorpion lived along the high-tide mark on the beaches of the Mexican peninsula of Baja California. Its record was for population density. Polis found that two to a dozen of these scorpions lived within any square meter of shore habitat. As Polis remarked, "It is not a good place to spread your sleeping bag."

Directions: Refer to the passage to answer the questions.

1. Which statement is true?
   a. All rattlesnakes are sidewinders.
   b. Some sidewinders are rattlesnakes.
   c. Most sidewinders are rattlesnakes.
   d. Some rattlesnakes are sidewinders.

2. Which statement is **not** true?
   a. Scorpions are sensitive to light.
   b. There are 1,500 scorpion species venomous enough to kill a human.
   c. Scorpions' natural habitat is the desert.
   d. Scorpions glow under ultraviolet light.

3. List the two things Polis did to prevent further injury from surprise snake encounters.

_____

_____

Another Dimension

Volume of a Rectangular Prism

A *prism* is a three-dimensional polygon with parallel sides and 90° angles. The formula for the volume of a rectangular prism is $V = l \times w \times h$.

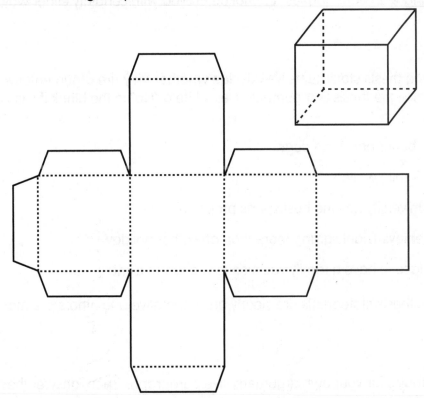

On the left is a *cubic inch*. It is one inch long, one inch wide, and one inch high.

Also on the left is the flat outline of a cubic inch.

Trace and cut out the outline along the black lines. Then fold along the dashed lines and tape in place.

Directions: Use the cubic inch you cut out and folded to do this activity. Estimate the number of cubic inches that would fit in the following objects.

1. pencil box = _____ cu. in.

2. table top = _____ cu. in.

3. book = _____ cu. in.

4. dictionary = _____ cu. in.

5. calculator = _____ cu. in.

6. toaster = _____ cu. in.

Find two other objects to estimate.

7. _____ = _____ cu. in.

8. _____ = _____ cu. in.

Challenge: Now measure these objects and use the following formula to see if you were right.

$$V = l \times w \times h$$
(**V**olume = **l**ength x **w**idth x **h**eight)

Being Argumentative

Some subjects are argumentative, and others are not. The thesis "In the United States, hurricanes have caused the most severe damage to families living in Florida" is not argumentative. It is either true or not true, and a bit of research can prove it one way or the other. However, a thesis such as "Hurricanes are more frightening than earthquakes" *cannot* be proved with certainty either way, and it is, therefore, argumentative.

Part I

Directions: Look at the following thesis statements and decide whether they are argumentative or not. Place an "A" in the blank if the thesis is argumentative. Write a "No" in the blank if it is not argumentative.

_____ 1. Cats make better pets than dogs.

_____ 2. Arizona has mild winters.

_____ 3. Our state university has the best sports program.

_____ 4. My family enjoys Thanksgiving more than any other holiday.

_____ 5. The best place to have a family vacation is in a warm climate.

You will notice that some of the thesis statements are clearly argumentative and others are more difficult to figure out.

Part II

Directions: Brainstorm some topics for your own argumentative paragraph. Then, answer the questions to finish your pre-write.

Choose a topic: _____

Choose a side to take on the issue: _____

Brainstorm some possible reasons for your argument: _____

_____

_____

Now to prove that this is truly an argumentative paragraph, how might someone else argue the other side? _____

_____

Challenge: Write your paragraph on a separate piece of paper and try it out. Did you manage to convince someone to agree with you?

Lifesaving Blood

Dr. Charles Drew was born in 1904 in Washington, D.C., the grandchild of African American, Native American, and white grandparents. He attended segregated schools where he was an excellent student and a successful athlete. As a teenager, he worked in factories and construction. The death of his sister from tuberculosis spurred his interest in becoming a medical <u>doctor</u>. He received a scholarship to Amherst College, where most of the students were white. He excelled in both football and his studies. Drew entered medical school at McGill University in Montreal, Canada. He graduated in 1933 with honors.

Drew became interested in the idea of <u>blood</u> <u>transfusions</u>. While getting an advanced degree in <u>medicine</u> from Columbia University, he kept researching how to <u>store</u> blood safely. He developed blood banks and special techniques to store blood and <u>plasma</u>. Part of the process required machines to separate plasma from red blood <u>cells</u>.

He worked with the <u>Red Cross</u> and British and American authorities to make his new methods available to thousands of <u>wounded</u> soldiers. Many people made blood <u>donations</u> to the Red Cross during World War II. Dr. Charles Drew died in an automobile accident in 1950, but his <u>contribution</u> to medicine has saved millions of lives in peacetime and in war.

Directions: After reading the passage, find and circle the underlined words in the word search below.

```
B  N  Q  I  C  O  A  F  R  C  W  O
T  R  A  N  S  F  U  S  I  O  N  S
N  O  Z  C  M  R  K  E  U  N  L  T
G  T  S  E  T  C  A  N  I  T  E  W
P  C  Y  N  B  Y  D  X  S  R  H  K
E  O  F  I  O  E  E  L  A  I  M  R
B  D  R  C  D  I  L  R  D  B  F  D
L  N  Z  I  J  E  T  K  O  U  E  Z
O  S  A  D  C  H  V  A  W  T  K  O
O  G  W  E  L  R  C  S  N  I  S  I
D  Y  A  M  S  A  L  P  L  O  G  Y
R  E  D  C  R  O  S  S  B  N  D  C
```

Stepping Into the Wilderness

Part I

Directions: The steps below offer advice on how to survive in the wilderness. As you read them, find the meaning of each underlined word and put the letter of the answer on the blank line. Use the definitions in the box below to help you.

> A. blank, empty
> B. to beat, hit hard
> C. sticky wetland
> (or troublesome situation)
>
> D. capable
> E. along a bank or shore
> F. hidden supply

_____ 1. First, set up your camp in a <u>riparian</u> area so that fishing is easily available.

_____ 2. Second, use the shelter of trees for your camp because a <u>stark</u> area gets too much sunshine.

_____ 3. Third, be sure that you are very <u>apt</u> at starting a campfire. You'll need it for heat and light.

_____ 4. Fourth, always have a heavy stick available in case you need to <u>drub</u> a snake.

_____ 5. Fifth, always be certain that you are walking on solid ground. To step in a <u>quagmire</u> would be dangerous!

_____ 6. Sixth, keep a <u>hoard</u> of food and water. Use it very carefully.

Part II

Directions: Complete each of the series below with one of your new words.

1. storehouse, stock, _____

2. mud, muck, _____

3. coastal, riverine, _____

4. able, qualified, _____

5. bare, nothing, _____

6. attack, strike, _____

Challenge: Create a journal entry on a separate sheet of paper, imagining that you are camping in the wilderness. Use as many of the vocabulary words as you can.

Locating Information

The Nile River

The Nile River is about four thousand miles long. It is considered the longest river in the world. The source, or start, of the river is in Ethiopia. The mouth, or end, of the river is the Mediterranean Sea. The Nile flows from south to north. The Nile River has a series of cataracts. A cataract is another name for a waterfall.

The Nile River is located in a part of the world that does not get a lot of rain. Much of the river flows through the Sahara Desert. But once every year, the areas that provide the Nile's water receive heavy rains. These rains make the Nile overflow. The water rises up over the river banks and floods the surrounding area. The ancient Egyptians would plant seeds and grow crops in the moist, fertile soil.

The ancient Egyptians grew many different kinds of crops in the Nile River Valley. They grew vegetables, wheat, and papyrus. Papyrus is a kind of plant that was used to make paper.

The ancient Egyptians figured out a way to irrigate their crops. They dug irrigation channels that directed the water from the Nile River to where it was needed.

It is unlikely that any civilization would have existed here if it were not for the Nile River.

Directions: Use the passage above to answer the questions.

1. Which paragraph states what a cataract is?
   - ⓐ paragraph 4
   - ⓑ paragraph 1
   - ⓒ paragraph 3
   - ⓓ paragraph 2

2. What event made it possible for the ancient Egyptians to grow crops?
   - ⓐ consistent rainfall
   - ⓑ fertile soil
   - ⓒ The Nile flooded its banks yearly.
   - ⓓ the plow

3. From what plant did the ancient Egyptians make paper?
   - ⓐ palm trees
   - ⓑ papyrus
   - ⓒ cottonwood
   - ⓓ reeds

4. Why was the Nile River important to the ancient Egyptians?
   - ⓐ They planted crops along the fertile riverbanks.
   - ⓑ It flows through the Sahara Desert.
   - ⓒ It has waterfalls.
   - ⓓ It is four thousand miles long.

5. The Nile River empties into
   - ⓐ Ethiopia.
   - ⓑ the Sahara Desert.
   - ⓒ Egypt.
   - ⓓ the Mediterranean Sea.

6. How did ancient Egyptians use natural resources in their daily lives?

   _____

   _____

   _____

Directions: The McNeil family spent five days of their vacation in Florida. They visited a different tourist attraction each day. Using the clues below, determine which day they visited each attraction. Use the chart, and cross out possibilities as you eliminate them. Put a check mark in the box that represents each correct answer.

	Tues.	Wed.	Thurs.	Fri.	Sat.
Blue Spring State Park					
SeaWorld®					
Epcot® theme park					
Universal Studios Florida®					
Orlando Science Center					

Clue 1: The McNeil family decided to go to SeaWorld before they went to Universal Studios Florida.

Clue 2: They decided to go to Epcot theme park the day after visiting Blue Spring State Park.

Clue 3: They went to Blue Spring State Park two days after visiting Universal Studios Florida.

All About Me

After completing the self-profile below, put it in a safe place so you can look back at it in a few years to see what has changed and what has stayed the same.

Date Completed: _____

Name: _____

Age: _____ Grade: _____

My favorite subject is _____

When I'm not at school, I like to _____

_____

_____

My closest friends are _____

_____

_____

When I go to college, I want to major in _____

_____

_____

Describe what you look like and what you like to wear. Give specific details.

_____

_____

_____

_____

_____

_____

Attach a photo of yourself here:

What do you want to tell your future self? _____

_____

_____

_____

Summer Reading List

○ **The Firegirl** by Tony Abbott

Tom befriends a new girl who is receiving treatments at the local hospital for disfiguring burns. Tom's friend wants nothing to do with her due to her altered appearance. Tom looks beyond the surface to support her.

Themes: acceptance, friendship

○ **The Book of Three** by Lloyd Alexander

Taran, a young pig-keeper, is dissatisfied with his life of farm labor. He longs for adventures like those he hears his caretaker read about in a book called *The Book of Three*. When the pig digs out of her pen and runs away, following her leads to a series of unforeseen events.

Themes: coming of age, humor, honor

○ **The Fighting Ground** by Avi

The popular children's author tells the tale of Jonathon, a thirteen-year-old who fights in the Revolutionary War. The boy soon finds that the real battle is within himself.

Themes: facing fear, humanity, values

○ **Who Cares?** by Krista Bell

Toby has a passion that he is afraid will earn him ridicule—dancing. Rhys has a much bigger secret—an alcoholic mother. Though at first they barely know each other, over a week of vacation, the two boys find acceptance and support in their new friendship.

Themes: friendship, family, identity

○ **Shark Girl** by Kelly Bingham

Jane has survived a shark attack. Her arm has been amputated, and she must go back to school and put her life back together. This book is written mostly in free verse.

Themes: healing, courage

○ **What happened to Serenity?** by P.J. Sarah Collins

In this dystopian novel, no one in Katherine's community is allowed to ask any questions. They are told how to live and what to feel. When a child in Katherine's community disappears, she can't forget about it as she is supposed to.

Themes: searching for truth, freedom

Making the Most of Summertime Reading

When reading these books, ask yourself the questions below. Answering these questions will enhance your reading comprehension skills.

○ Why did you choose this book to read?

○ Name a character from the story that you like. Why do you like him or her?

○ Where does the story take place? Would you want to vacation there?

○ Name a problem that occurs in the story. How is it resolved?

○ What is the best part of the story so far? Describe it!

○ What do you think is going to happen next in the story? Make a prediction!

○ Who are the important characters in the story? Why are they important?

○ Would you tell your friend to read this book? Why or why not?

When you finish a book, write a book review (page 106). The questions above can help you decide what to write.

Summer Reading List (cont.)

☼ **Waiting for Normal** by Leslie Connor

Addie is looking for a normal life while living with her irresponsible mother in a trailer in upstate New York. This book has humor, tension, and well-developed characters.

Themes: looking for the positive, dysfunctional parent, endurance

☼ **Mockingbird** by Kathryn Erskine

In this National Book Award winner, Caitlin, a young girl with Asperger's, has always relied on her brother to guide her through the perplexities of life. Now, her brother has been killed in a tragic school shooting and Caitlin must find a way to gain closure and navigate her life without him.

Themes: school violence, grief, family

☼ **Inkheart** by Cornelia Funke

Meggie lives alone with her father, a bookbinder, who has the "gift" of reading aloud and bringing the characters to life—literally. When Dustfinger comes to life on a dark and stormy night, their quiet lives change forever.

Themes: family, courage

☼ **Rapunzel's Revenge** by Shannon Hale

This graphic novel retells the famous fairy tale in a Wild West setting. Rapunzel escapes the home her mother has turned into a prison and vows to destroy the evil empire with the help of her hair!

Themes: humor, adventure, heroism

☼ **Redwall** by Brian Jacques

Cluny, the evil rat warlord, prepares to fight for the ownership of Redwall Abbey. The young mouse Mattias vows to recover the lost sword of Martin the Warrior, the only weapon that can save the abbey from Cluny. Strong ties with local animals, along with the magic of the sword, enable Matthias to defeat Cluny.

Themes: courage, adventure, good vs. evil

☼ **The Worst-Case Scenario Ultimate Adventure: Mars** by Hena Khan and David Borgenicht with Robert Zubrin

In this choose-your-own-adventure style nonfiction book, readers explore space travel and colonize Mars. This book challenges readers to make good decisions as they try to survive this unique adventure.

Themes: space travel, active learning

☼ **Day of Tears** by Julius Lester

This is a historical novel about the largest slave auction in United States history. The author uses dialogue and monologue to tell the story of Emma, a slave, and her owner, Pierce Butler. Emma wants to teach Pierce's daughters kindness, and Pierce wants to protect his assets.

Themes: injustice, caring for others

❖ **The Boneshaker** by Kate Milford

Thirteen-year-old Natalie Minks loves machines. Jake Limberleg comes to town with his traveling medicine show. Natalie senses something is not quite right about Jake and his healers. She investigates the medicine show and discovers that her knowledge of automata and other machines gives her the ability to set things right. Set in Missouri in the early 20th century.

Themes: family, courage, community

❖ **Cuba 15** by Nancy Osa

Violet's Cuban grandmother insists on a 15th-year celebration for Violet—a traditional Quinceañera. Violet is reluctant at first, but then she learns that the celebration is about tradition and family. In preparation for the event, Violet probes into her Cuban roots and unwittingly unleashes a hotbed of conflicted feelings about Cuba within her family. She secretly participates in a rally for Cuba, inspiring great anger and division in her family, who lived through the political strife there. Set in suburban Chicago.

Themes: self-discovery, growing up, family traditions, friendship, acceptance

❖ **The Hunchback Assignments** by Arthur Slade

Mr. Socrates rescues young Modo, a hunchback, from a traveling freak show. Modo has the ability to transform his shape to reflect another person. Socrates trains Modo to become a secret agent for the Permanent Association, which strives to protect the country from evil. Fourteen-year-old Modo is then turned loose in Victorian London to fend for himself.

Themes: survival, heroism

❖ **After Ever After** by Jordan Sonnenblick

Eighth grader Jeffrey's cancer is in remission, and he finds life still offers plenty of struggles. In his words, "Treatment is nothing compared to what happens after you've been 'cured.' . . . Being a cancer survivor can be a life sentence all its own." This humorous and hopeful story explores what happens when you stop surviving and start to live again.

Themes: survival, abandonment issues, special needs

❖ **Maniac Magee** by Jerry Spinelli

This Newbery Award-winning book chronicles a resourceful orphan who must make his own way in the world after running away from an impossible living situation.

Themes: race relationships, making the best of bad situations, hope

❖ **American Born Chinese** by Gene Yang

This award-winning graphic novel contains three interwoven tales. One of the central characters is Jin Wang, a Chinese American who wants to fit in and win the respect of more popular boys. He struggles with how his family and ethnicity differ from more "American" ideals.

Themes: identity, personal growth

Fun Ways to Love Books

Here are some fun ways that your child can expand on his or her reading. The wording has been directed towards your child because we want him or her to be inspired to love books.

Write to the Author

Many authors love to hear from their readers, especially when they hear what people liked best about their books. You can write to an author and send your letter in care of the book's publisher. The publisher's address is listed directly after the title page. Or you may go to the author's website and follow the directions for how to send the author a letter or email. (To make sure your author is still living, do a search on the Internet by typing the author's name into a search engine.)

A Comic Book or Graphic Novel

Turn your favorite book into a comic book or graphic novel. Fold at least two sheets of paper in half, and staple them so they make a book. With a ruler and pencil, draw boxes across each page to look like blank comic strips. Then draw the story of your book as if it were a comic. Draw pictures of your characters, and have words coming out of their mouths—just as in a real comic strip. You can also find free comic-making programs online.

Always Take a Book

Maybe you've had to wait with your parents in line at the post office or in the vet's waiting room with nothing to do. If you get into the habit of bringing a book with you wherever you go, you'll always have something exciting to do! Train yourself to always take a good book. You might want to carry a small backpack or shoulder bag—something that allows you to carry a book easily from place to place. Don't forget a bookmark!

Novel Foods

What foods do the characters in your books eat? What do they drink? What are their favorite foods? Get a better sense of your character's tastes by cooking their favorite foods. Some characters love sweet things, like cookies and ice cream. Other characters like hamburgers and pizza. Decide what foods your characters love. Locate appropriate recipes on the Internet or in books. Then make up a grocery list. Buy groceries and gather necessary materials, such as mixing bowls, spoons, and pans. Cook your characters' favorite foods with your family and friends.

Write a Sequel

What happens to the characters in your book after you finish reading the final page? Why not create a sequel? A sequel is a book that is published after the first book has enjoyed success among readers. Sequels generally pick up where the first book left off. For example, the sequel to Madeleine L'Engle's novel *A Wrinkle in Time* is *A Wind in the Door.*

Graph Paper

Name: _____ Activity Name: _____

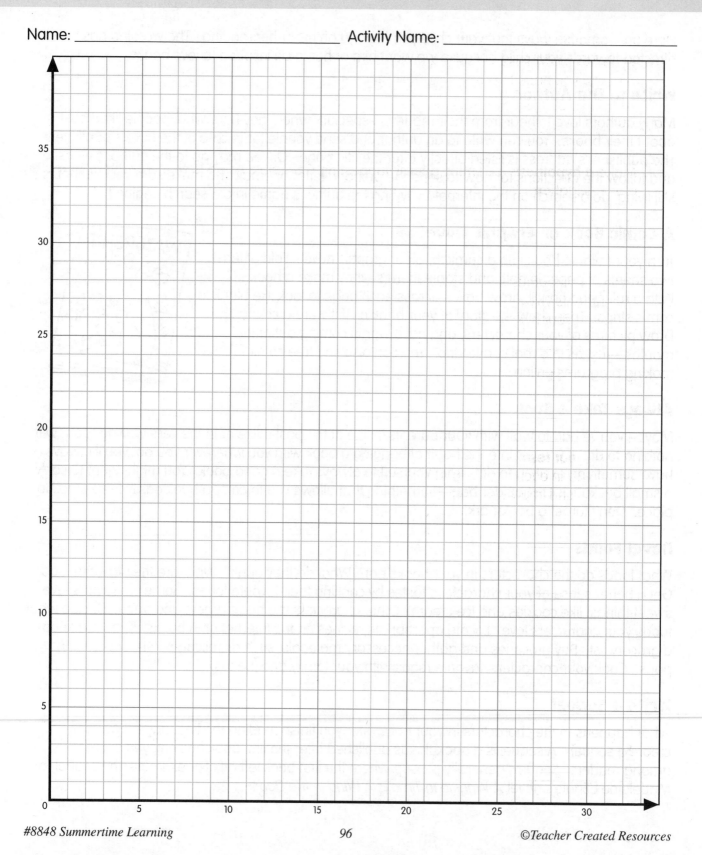

Science Investigation Worksheet

Your child can use this page while exploring the world around him or her this summer.

I. State the problem to be solved or investigated. (What is the purpose of your investigation? What do you hope to prove, demonstrate, or find out?)

_____

_____

_____

II. Make a hypothesis (scientific guess) suggesting a possible solution to the problem or a plan of investigation. (What do you think is actually going to happen?)

_____

_____

_____

III. Test your hypothesis using experimentation, models, and other investigations. (What experiments will you try? What models are you going to make? What are you actually going to do to test your hypothesis?)

_____

_____

_____

_____

_____

IV. Record your results. (Keep an accurate, detailed, and complete record here of what happened in each investigation. Tell what happened and when it happened. Describe any changes and improvements you made. Draw pictures of the model or project.)

_____

_____

_____

_____

Illustration:

V. State your conclusions. (Tell what you learned.)

_____

_____

Journal Topics

Choose one of these journal topics each day. Make sure you add enough detail so someone else reading it will clearly be able to know at least four of the following:

☆ **who**   ☆ **what**   ☆ **when**   ☆ **where**   ☆ **why**   ☆ **how**

1. If I had a pen pal in Australia or India (or another country), I would ask him or her . . .
2. If I could get a job after school, I would like to . . .
3. One activity I do well and could explain to someone else is . . .
4. I would (or would not) like to be a doctor because . . .
5. If I were going to interview the president of the United States or the leader of another country, the one question I would be sure to ask is . . .
6. If I were on a committee to improve health and reduce the amount of obesity in adolescents, I would suggest . . .
7. If I own a business when I grow up, it will be . . .
8. If I could build my own house anywhere I wanted, I would choose . . .
9. If I went on vacation and could choose to stay in a hotel or go camping, I would . . .
10. The perfect way to eat ice cream is . . .
11. When we help other people, we benefit by . . .
12. In ten years, I will be . . .
13. If we suddenly had no electricity, I would . . .
14. One person who has made a big impression on me is _____ because . . .
15. If I won an award, I would want it to be for . . .
16. My life as a popular sports figure would be . . .
17. If I could migrate to another place, I would go . . .
18. I would like to be (or would not like to be) a writer or artist because . . .
19. An event in my life that would make a good book is . . .
20. Sometimes it is okay (or not okay) to end a friendship because . . .
21. A choice I have made that affected my life is . . .
22. The most creative thing I have ever made is . . .
23. One television show worth watching is _____ because . . .
24. If I had to choose the college I would attend right now, it would be . . .
25. A perfect summer day would be . . .

Learning Experiences

Here are some fun, low-cost activities that you can do with your child. You'll soon discover that these activities can be stimulating, educational, and complementary to the other exercises in this book.

How Much Does It Cost?

If you go out for a meal, have your child total the bill. Have your child either use a hand-held calculating device or write down the cost of each person's meal. Then have him or her add it all together, find the total, and then figure tax and tip. You can also have your child figure out the average cost of each meal.

Travel Journals

If you are going away during the summer, have your child keep a journal. In the journal, he or she can describe favorite parts of the trip or skills and wisdom gained. Encourage your child to include evidence, such as photos and other graphic items. The look and format of the journal can depend on your child's preferences and personality. One option is for your child to collect postcards or take photographs, paste them into a blank journal, and write captions for each one.

The Big Outdoors

Spend some time outdoors with your child. If you live near mountains, learn about them with a bit of research beforehand. What type of mountains are they? How were they formed? What type of vegetation do they support? Then take a hike. Or go to a beach, lake, or park. Pack a picnic lunch and lots of water. Do some exploring and, best of all, talk about it. Discuss how people have affected the environment and how different environments affect the way people do things.

Project Pantry

Find a place in your house where you can store supplies. This might be a closet or a bin that stays in one spot. Get some clean paint cans or buckets. Fill them with all types of craft and art supplies. Besides the typical paints, markers, paper, scissors, and glue, include some more unusual things, such as tiles, salt dough, artificial flowers, boxes or other small containers, objects from nature, and wrapping paper. You can buy supplies, or you can repurpose items found around the house. This way, whenever your child wants to do a craft project, he or she will have everything needed at that moment. For example, your child can create a diorama to depict an important scene in a favorite book or movie. Or, your child can make a gift for a family member or someone in need.

Build Something

Build something with your child. This might be a bench, a small table, or a birdhouse. You'll need to collect tools, nails, screws, paint, or anything else you might need. There are many suggestions on the Internet, in magazines, or at do-it-yourself home stores. Decide if you are going to do a ready-made project, find directions and follow them, or be totally original. Encourage your child to use his or her math skills. The possibilities are endless.

Websites

Math Websites

☼ **AAA Math:** http://www.aaamath.com/
This site contains hundreds of pages of basic math skills divided by grade or topic.

☼ **AllMath.com:** http://www.allmath.com/
This site has metric conversions, biographies of mathematicians, a math glossary, and a link to *Ask Dr. Math*.

☼ **BrainBashers:** http://www.brainbashers.com/
This is a unique collection of brainteasers, games, and optical illusions.

☼ **Coolmath.com:** http://www.coolmath.com/
Explore this amusement park of mathematics! Have fun with the interactive activities.

☼ **Mrs. Glosser's Math Goodies:** http://www.mathgoodies.com/
This is a free, educational site featuring interactive worksheets, puzzles, and more!

Reading and Writing Websites

☼ **Aesop's Fables:** http://www.umass.edu/aesop/
This site has almost forty of the fables. Both traditional and modern versions are presented.

☼ **American Library Association:** http://ala.org/
Visit this site to find out both the past and present John Newbery Medal and Randolph Caldecott Medal winners.

☼ **Book Adventure:** http://www.bookadventure.com/
This site features a free reading incentive program dedicated to encouraging children in grades K-8 to read.

☼ **Graphic Organizers:** http://www.eduplace.com/graphicorganizer/
Use these graphic organizers to help your child think about what he or she reads and also to write in an organized manner.

☼ **ReadWriteThink:** http://www.readwritethink.org/
Find interactive pages, parent and after-school resources, and lesson plans on this site.

☼ **Wacky Web Tales:** http://www.eduplace.com/tales/index.html
This is a great place for budding writers to submit their stories and read other children's writing.

☼ **Write on Reader:** http://library.thinkquest.org/J001156/
Children can visit *Write on Reader* to gain a love of reading and writing.

☼ **The Internet Public Library:** http://www.ipl.org/
This site offers a wealth of resources for research, reading, writing and more. A free "ask a librarian" service is also available.

Websites *(cont.)*

Science and Social Studies Websites

☼ **Animal Photos:** http://nationalzoo.si.edu/
This site offers wonderful pictures of animals, as well as virtual zoo visits.

☼ **Animal Planet:** http://animal.discovery.com/
Children can watch videos or play games at this site for animal lovers.

☼ **Dinosaur Guide:** http://dsc.discovery.com/dinosaurs/
This is an interactive site on dinosaurs that goes beyond just learning about the creatures.

☼ **The Electronic Zoo:** http://netvet.wustl.edu/e-zoo.htm
This site has links to thousands of animal sites covering every creature under the sun!

☼ **Great Buildings Online:** http://www.greatbuildings.com/
This gateway to architecture around the world and across history documents a thousand buildings and hundreds of leading architects.

☼ **Mr. Dowling's Electronic Passport:** http://www.mrdowling.com/index.html
This is an incredible history and geography site.

☼ **NASA Studies:** http://kids.earth.nasa.gov/
Click on "Natural Hazards" for an in-depth look at hurricanes, from how they're created to how dangerous they are. This site also has links for climate studies, experts, and other resources.

☼ **Natural Inquirer:** http://www.naturalinquirer.org/
This is a middle school science education journal that has articles and resources on various topics.

☼ **U.S. Environmental Protection Agency:** http://www.epa.gov/students/
Explore this site for lessons, resources, and links to games, videos, and quizzes about environmental education.

☼ **WiseGeek:** http://www.wisegeek.com/
This site has "clear answers for common questions." Easy-to-use question search format includes language, humanities, and science articles.

☼ **National Geographic:** http://www.nationalgeographic.com/
Have fun learning about our planet with games, videos, and articles about animals, countries, and other topics.

☼ **America's Story from America's Library:** http://www.americaslibrary.gov/
Explore U.S. history using primary sources from the Library of Congress. Kids can discover America's story, meet amazing Americans, and explore the states.

☼ **Smithsonian:** http://www.si.edu/kids/
Explore the various Smithsonian museums online with activities, fun facts, games, and links to learn about influential Americans.

Commonly Misspelled Words

Here are some of the most commonly misspelled words in the English language. Use this list to help you spell the words correctly.

a lot	height	pronounce
a while	heroes	realize
accept	immediate	receipt
advice	independent	receive
argument	intelligence	recommend
believe	judgment	reference
calendar	length	relevant
changeable	library	rhyme
choose	light	rhythm
commitment	medieval	schedule
committed	millennium	seize
conscience	mischievous	sentence
definitely	misspell	separate
dependent	naturally	similar
dictionary	necessary	succeed
easily	neighbor	temperature
embarrass	night	their
exceed	no one	tomorrow
excellence	noticeable	twelfth
existence	occasionally	unique
experience	opinion	usually
explanation	opportunity	vacuum
familiar	perseverance	valuable
fascinating	personal	visible
February	piece	weather
finally	possession	Wednesday
foreign	prejudice	weird
grateful	privilege	writing
happily	proceed	young

Proofreading Marks

Editor's Mark	Meaning	Example
≡	capitalize	they fished in lake tahoe.
/	make it lowercase	Five $tudents missed the $us.
sp.	spelling mistake	The day was clowdy and cold.
⊙	add a period	Tomorrow is a holiday⊙
ℒ	delete (remove)	One person knew the the answer.
∧	add a word	Six were in the litter.
⋀	add a comma	He planted peas corn, and squash.
∽	reverse words or letters	An otter swam in the bed kelp.
∨	add an apostrophe	The child's bike was blue.
∨ ∨	add quotation marks	Why can't I go? she cried.
#	make a space	He ate two redapples.
◡	close the space	Her favorite game is soft ball.
⌗	begin a new paragraph	to know. Next on the list

Measurement Tools

Measurement Charts

millimeters (mm)	1	10	1,000	1,000,000
centimeters (cm)	1/10	1	100	100,000
meters (m)	1/1,000	1/100	1	1,000
kilometers (km)	1/1,000,000	1/100,000	1/1,000	1

inches (in.)	1	12	36	63,360
feet (ft.)	1/12	1	3	5,280
yards (yd.)	1/36	1/3	1	1,760
miles (mi.)	1/63,360	1/5,280	1/1,760	1

cups (c.)	1	2	4	8	16
pints (pt.)	1/2	1	2	4	8
quarts (qt.)	1/4	1/2	1	2	4
gallons (gal.)	1/16	1/8	1/4	1/2	1

Temperature

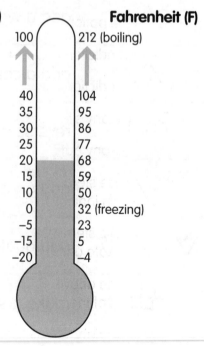

Celsius (C)　　　Fahrenheit (F)

Celsius	Fahrenheit
100	212 (boiling)
40	104
35	95
30	86
25	77
20	68
15	59
10	50
0	32 (freezing)
−5	23
−15	5
−20	−4

Conversion Facts

1 in. = 2.54 cm
1 yd. = 0.9144 m
1 mi. = 1.609344 km
1 c. = 236.588237 ml

Temperature Conversion

To Fahrenheit (F)	To Celcius (C)
$(C \times 9/5) + 32$	$(F - 32) \times 5/9$

Test-Taking Tips

The Secrets to Acing Tests!

- ☼ Attend school regularly and be on time.
- ☼ Come to school prepared, rested and ready to learn.
- ☼ Complete all of your classroom and homework assignments.
- ☼ Ask for help if you don't understand.
- ☼ Spend time every day studying and reviewing material.
- ☼ Create an organized and quiet place in which to study.
- ☼ Know that procrastination is the enemy of achievement!

Multiple-Choice Strategies

1. Read the question carefully.

2. Cover the options and make a prediction.

3. If your prediction or something close to it appears, select it.

4. If your prediction does not appear, read each option carefully.

5. Eliminate any silly options.

6. Eliminate any options you know to be incorrect.

7. A sentence stem and an option that together create a grammatically incorrect statement may be an indication that it is wrong.

8. Preface the stem and option choice with the phrase "It is true that. . ." If the stem and option create a true statement, it is an indication that it is correct.

9. If "All of the above" is an option and at least two of the other options are correct, then select "All of the above".

10. If "All of the above" is an option and you know that at least one of the options is wrong, then eliminate both "All of the above" and the other incorrect option.

11. If "None of the above" is an option and at least one of the options is correct, then eliminate "None of the above" as a possibility.

Book Review

Before they purchase a book online, many people read the reviews written by other readers. Write a review of a book you read in the space provided below. Be sure to support your opinion with at least three specific reasons you feel that way.

Book Title: _____

Author: _____

Star Rating: ☆ ☆ ☆ ☆ ☆

Review: _____

_____

_____

_____

_____

_____

_____

_____

_____

_____

_____

_____

_____

_____

_____

_____

_____

I would/would not recommend this book to a friend.

Reviewed by: _____

Answer Key

Page 12
1. c
2. a
3. 4 = date in August that Woodruff ran
   1936 = year he ran in the Olympic Games
   21 = Woodruff's age when he made Olympic team
   6'3" = Woodruff's height
   10 = length in feet of Woodruff's stride when extended
   1:52.9 = Woodruff's victory time (1 minute, 52.9 seconds)

Page 15
Part I
Rule: Multiply input by 2
540 sq. ft., $1,080
600 sq. ft., $1,200
660 sq. ft., $1,320
720 sq. ft., $1,440
780 sq. ft., $1,560
1. Answers will vary.
2. Yes

Part II
100 ft., $150
200 ft., $300
300 ft., $450
400 ft., $600
500 ft., $750
1. $600.00
2. $225.00

Page 16
Part I
1. salvage
2. tamper
3. decrepit
4. assure
5. reserve
6. furnish

Challenge
1. reserve
2. assure
3. furnish

Part II
1. decrepit
2. salvage
3. reserve
4. furnish
5. tamper
6. assure

4. decrepit
5. tamper
6. salvage

Page 17
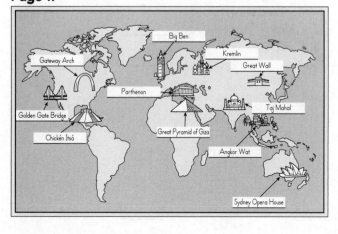

Page 18
1. a   2. b   3. c   4. d

Page 19
1. d   2. c   3. a   4. b   5. c   6. b

Page 20
clever feline — witty kitty
bashful insect — shy fly
obese feline — fat cat
minor car crash — fender bender
large swine — big pig
ill hen — sick chick
little snack — light bite
enjoyable jogging — fun run
soaked dog — wet pet
bloody tale — gory story
ailing bloodsucker — sick tick
light red beverage — pink drink
comical rabbit — funny bunny
unhappy boy — sad lad

Page 21
Part I
March — 90
April — 25
May — 70
June — 25
July — 45
August — 45
Part II
Mr. Sanders — $5,900
Ms. Elliott — $2,400
Mrs. Shaw — $6,400
Mr. Smitz — $2,900

Page 24
1. a   2. b   3. d   4. b

Page 25
1. a. given
   b. 6 in 12 or 1 in 2 (1:2, 1/2)
   c. 6 in 12 or 1 in 2 (1:2, 1/2)
   d. 5 in 12 (5:12, 5/12)
   e. 7 in 12 (7:12, 7/12)
   f. 10 in 12 or 5 in 6 (5:6, 5/6)
2. a. 5 in 20 or 1 in 4 (1:4, 1/4)
   b. 4 in 20 or 1 in 5 (1:5, 1/5)
   c. 16 in 20 or 4 in 5 (4:5, 4/5)
   d. 0
Remaining answers may vary.

Answer Key (cont.)

Page 27
References to the three types of geologic plate boundaries should be marked on the page.

Page 28
1. d
2. a
3. Answers will vary.

Page 29
1. d   2. c   3. a   4. a   5. b   6. c

Page 30
1. O
2. F
3. N
4. U
5. A
6. H
7. Y
8. T
9. C
10. K
11. I

"You can if you think you can."

Page 31
1. 694.64 sq. meters
2. 3 hours and 20 minutes
3. 900 sq. meters
4. 10 hours and 30 minutes
5. Divided the answer to problem 3 by 10, and multiplied the result by 7
6. 75 bags

Page 32
Part I
1. confound
2. mustang
3. wallow
4. colossal
5. critters
6. inception

Part II
1. confound
2. wallow
3. mustang
4. colossal
5. inception
6. critters

Part III
1. d
2. c

Page 33
1. d
2. a
3. (1) The orca signals other members of pod.
   (2) The orca swims underneath floe.
   (4) The orca pushes floe up so animals slide down.

Page 35
A = $8
B = $25
C = $14
D = $32
E = $22
F = $31
G = $26
H = $15
I = $7
J = $5
Picture: candle

Page 36
1. c
2. a
Remaining answers will vary.

Page 38
Possible answers include:
1. If I had an opportunity to go anywhere in the world, I would choose Italy.
   If I had an opportunity to go anywhere in the world, I would just visit the northern part of my state.
2. The most beautiful season is winter, when the snow makes the whole city clean and white.
   My favorite season is summer, when there is no school.
3. Taking care of older family members who need help is the responsibility of everyone.
   As a child, I loved to spend time with my grandmother and hear fascinating stories of her childhood.

Page 39
1. a. $1,453.35
   b. Bargain Movers
   c. You Do It
2. Friday
3. $B = 2P - 3$

Answer Key *(cont.)*

Page 40
1. vegetables that grow underground
2. citrus fruits
3. fruits that begin with the letter P
4. months with 30 days
5. types of clouds
6. members of the cat family
7. mythical creatures
8. ground transportation
9. states that border the Gulf of Mexico
10. states that border the Atlantic Ocean
11. states that border Mexico

Page 41
1. 2:43
2. 1952
3. a. CDXVII NE CXLVIII Avenue
   b. MCMXLIV NE LII Street

Page 43

Page 44
Part I
1. d
2. e
3. a
4. f
5. c
6. b

Part II
1. precipice
2. hillocks
3. infantry
4. cudgel
5. missive
6. aesthetic

Page 45
1. a. 3¾ cups trail mix total
   b. Each person will have 1¼ cup trail mix.
2. a. Each boy needs $66.66 for his share.
   b. Andrew needs to save $41.66 more.
3. a. $10.47
   b. $3.49
   c. Answers will vary.
4. a. 207
   b. 69

Page 48
1. d
2. Answers will vary.

Page 49
1. d   2. a   3. d   4. 40

Page 50
1. sharp
2. share
3. care
4. cart
5. chart
6. charm
7. hard
8. hare
9. fare
10. farm
11. alarm
12. lark
13. bark
14. dark
15. dare
16. date
17. late
18. lane
19. cane
20. cone

Page 51
Party Fruit Salad
Serves 24 people
18 cups watermelon
6 cups raisins
9 apples
1 ½ cups cherries
3 mangoes
Chili
Rule: Divided by 2 or Multiply by ½.
Serves 3 people
4 oz. cooked black beans
8 oz. cooked kidney beans
⅙ tsp. fresh garlic
¹⁄₁₀ lbs. snap peas
½ package chili powder
½ cup salsa

Answer Key (cont.)

Page 52
1. d
2. c
3. 1425: Aztecs conquered Totonacs
   1519: Cortes offered chocolate with vanilla by Aztecs
   1602: Morgan discovers vanilla flavor in own right
   1785: Jefferson is minister to France
   1801-09: Jefferson is U.S. president

Page 55
Jose Lasher likes almond.
Paul Sposito likes vanilla.
Borris Murphy likes chocolate.
Emanuel West likes strawberry.
Henry Herr likes peppermint.

Page 56
1. c   2. b   3. Drawings will vary.

Page 57

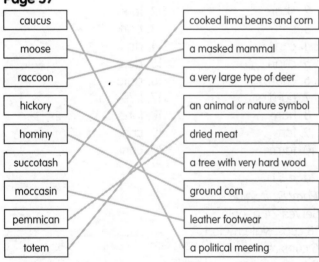

Challenge
Alabama	Massachusetts	Oklahoma
Alaska	Michigan	Oregon
Arizona	Minnesota	South Dakota
Arkansas	Mississippi	Tennessee
Connecticut	Missouri	Texas
Illinois	Nebraska	Utah
Iowa	New Mexico	Wisconsin
Kansas	North Dakota	Wyoming
Kentucky	Ohio	

Page 58
1. a   5. d
2. b   6. c
3. d   7. b
4. c   8. a

Page 59
1. b
2. "There are many significant positive reasons parents should think about that make teenage driving an important experience for maturing."
3. c

Page 60
1. man overboard
2. tricycle
3. holy cow
4. checkup
5. long time, no see
6. one in a million
7. split decision
8. touchdown
9. GI overseas

Page 61
Part I
Answers will vary.
Part II
1. 10
2. 100
3. 1,000
4. Answers will vary.
Part III
1. a diamond cutter
2. Answers will vary.

Part IV
1. 21
2. 360
3. no
4. 90
5. the distance around the outside of a shape

Page 65
A = 19   F = 22
B = 13   G = 27
C = 29   H = 16
D = 5   I = 15
E = 24   J = 12
Picture: windmill

Page 67
1. only one type of atom
2. two or more elements
3. Answers will vary.

Answer Key *(cont.)*

Page 69
Only consider each answer correct if adequate work is shown.

1. a   2. c   3. b

Page 70
1. Avi
2. Judy Blume
3. R. L. Stine
4. Beverly Cleary
5. Roald Dahl
6. J. K. Rowling
7. Dr. Seuss
8. Gary Paulsen
9. E. B. White
10. J. R. R. Tolkein
11. Mark Twain
12. Lois Lowry

Page 71
1. b
2. a
3. a
4. c
5. d

Page 72
1. a
2. b
3. Setting: Thailand, king's palace
   Characters: king, four counselors, farmer
   Problem: award only given for lie, counselors say everything true
   Results: if deemed true, gets money; if false, gets gold and princess

Page 73
obsidian — I
mudstone — S
sandstone — S
quartzite — M
pumice — I
marble — M
granite — I
rock salt — S

Page 75
There is more than one correct way to write each equation.

1. $72,450 - $65,000 = x, x = $7,450
2. $76,000 - $63,980 = x, x - $12,020
3. ($72,450 + $76,000)/20 = x, x = 7,423 bags (rounded)

Page 76
Part I

1. D	4. E
2. B	5. C
3. F	6. A

Part II

the opposite of "untangle" → entwine
cities more so than towns → populous
the opposite of "unremarkable" → momentous
faster than a jog → lope
smoother than a trail → boulevard
the opposite of being free → incarcerated

Challenge:
1. Alcatraz
2. Brazil
3. Lake Michigan
4. Arlington National Cemetery
5. Shetland Island
6. Gobi Desert

Page 77
1. b   2. b

Page 79
1. b   2. c   3. a   4. a

Page 80
Part I
2. cot + ton = cotton
3. pea + nut = peanut
4. sea + son = season

Remaining answers will vary.

Page 81

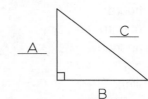

$$A^2 + B^2 = C^2$$
$$3^2 + 4^2 = 5^2$$
$$9 + 16 = 25$$

Page 83
Answers will vary.

·· —· ···· · ·— — ——— ·—·

I N V E N T O R

Answer Key *(cont.)*

Page 84
1. d
2. b
3. caught rattlesnakes in the area and sprayed them with paint that glowed under UV light
   wore chaps made of woven brass metal

Page 86
Part I
1. A   4. no
2. no   5. A
3. A
Part II
Answers will vary.

Page 87

```
B  N  Q  I  C  O  A  F  R  C  W  O
T  R  A  N  S  F  U  S  I  O  N  S
N  O  Z  C  M  R  K  E  U  N  L  T
G  T  S  E  T  C  A  N  I  T  E  W
P  C  Y  N  B  Y  D  X  S  R  H  K
E  O  F  I  O  E  E  L  A  I  M  R
B  D  R  C  D  I  L  R  D  B  F  D
L  N  Z  I  J  E  T  K  O  U  E  Z
O  S  A  D  C  H  V  A  W  T  K  O
O  G  W  E  L  R  C  S  N  I  S  I
D  Y  A  M  S  A  L  P  L  O  G  Y
R  E  D  C  R  O  S  S  B  N  D  C
```

Page 88

Part I	*Part II*
1. e	1. hoard
2. a	2. quagmire
3. d	3. riparian
4. b	4. apt
5. c	5. stark
6. f	6. drub

Page 89
1. b   4. a
2. c   5. d
3. b   6. Answers will vary.

Page 90
Tuesday — Sea World
Wednesday — Universal Studios Florida
Thursday — Orlando Science Center
Friday — Blue Spring State Park
Saturday — Epcot theme park

Answer Key (cont.)

Page 69

Only consider each answer correct if adequate work is shown.

1. a   2. c   3. b

Page 70

1. Avi
2. Judy Blume
3. R. L. Stine
4. Beverly Cleary
5. Roald Dahl
6. J. K. Rowling
7. Dr. Seuss
8. Gary Paulsen
9. E. B. White
10. J. R. R. Tolkein
11. Mark Twain
12. Lois Lowry

Page 71

1. b
2. a
3. a
4. c
5. d

Page 72

1. a
2. b
3. Setting: Thailand, king's palace
   Characters: king, four counselors, farmer
   Problem: award only given for lie, counselors say everything true
   Results: if deemed true, gets money; if false, gets gold and princess

Page 73

obsidian — I
mudstone — S
sandstone — S
quartzite — M
pumice — I
marble — M
granite — I
rock salt — S

Page 75

There is more than one correct way to write each equation.

1. $72,450 - $65,000 = x, x = $7,450
2. $76,000 - $63,980 = x, x - $12,020
3. ($72,450 + $76,000)/20 = x, x = 7,423 bags (rounded)

Page 76

Part I

1. D   4. E
2. B   5. C
3. F   6. A

Part II

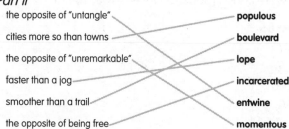

the opposite of "untangle" — entwine
cities more so than towns — populous
the opposite of "unremarkable" — momentous
faster than a jog — lope
smoother than a trail — boulevard
the opposite of being free — incarcerated

Challenge:

1. Alcatraz
2. Brazil
3. Lake Michigan
4. Arlington National Cemetery
5. Shetland Island
6. Gobi Desert

Page 77

1. b   2. b

Page 79

1. b   2. c   3. a   4. a

Page 80

Part I

2. cot + ton = cotton
3. pea + nut = peanut
4. sea + son = season

Remaining answers will vary.

Page 81

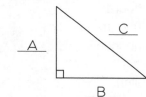

$$A^2 + B^2 = C^2$$
$$3^2 + 4^2 = 5^2$$
$$9 + 16 = 25$$

Page 83

Answers will vary.

INVENTOR

Answer Key (cont.)

Page 84
1. d
2. b
3. caught rattlesnakes in the area and sprayed them with paint that glowed under UV light
   wore chaps made of woven brass metal

Page 86
Part I
1. A
2. no
3. A
4. no
5. A

Part II
Answers will vary.

Page 87

```
B  N  Q  I  C  O  A  F  R  C  W  O
T  R  A  N  S  F  U  S  I  O  N  S
N  O  Z  C  M  R  K  E  U  N  L  T
G  T  S  E  T  C  A  N  I  T  E  W
P  C  Y  N  B  Y  D  X  S  R  H  K
E  O  F  I  O  E  E  L  A  I  M  R
B  D  R  C  D  I  L  R  D  B  F  D
L  N  Z  I  J  E  T  K  O  U  E  Z
O  S  A  D  C  H  V  A  W  T  K  O
O  G  W  E  L  R  C  S  N  I  S  I
D  Y  A  M  S  A  L  P  L  O  G  Y
R  E  D  C  R  O  S  S  B  N  D  C
```

Page 88
Part I
1. e
2. a
3. d
4. b
5. c
6. f

Part II
1. hoard
2. quagmire
3. riparian
4. apt
5. stark
6. drub

Page 89
1. b
2. c
3. b
4. a
5. d
6. Answers will vary.

Page 90
Tuesday — Sea World
Wednesday — Universal Studios Florida
Thursday — Orlando Science Center
Friday — Blue Spring State Park
Saturday — Epcot theme park